RESPONSIBLE

Responsible: A Memoir

Published by Gatekeeper Press
2167 Stringtown Rd, Suite 109
Columbus, OH 43123-2989
www.GatekeeperPress.com

ISBN (paperback): 9781642379136
eISBN: 9781642379143

RESPONSIBLE

A Memoir

Diana Hendel

gatekeeper press

Columbus, Ohio

This is a work of non-fiction.
I have not created any characters or composites,
but some of the names of people and
places have been changed.

Contents

---◆---

"Retrospectoscope: *n* — «*The view through scopes —
colonoscopes, arthroscopes and laparoscopes, to name a
few — routinely aids physicians in narrowing diagnoses
and arriving at a plan of care. But none is as illuminating
as the one doctors refer to as the "retrospectoscope," the
scope of hindsight. The retrospectoscope brings startling
clarity to the most mysterious disease processes: difficult
decisions become brilliant choices, minor missteps turn
into devastating errors, and the best of intentions can
transform into deep regret and persistent what-ifs.*»"

~ "*From Medical School to Middle Age*"
By Pauline W. Chen
From the New York Times
April 7, 2009

---◆---

Author's Note
Through the Retrospectoscope

IN THE SPRING OF 2017, I was invited to give the Commencement Address at my alma mater. As a former hospital CEO and a seasoned executive, I represented one example of achievement and success. I'd gone out into the world and "made it" and was, 28 years later, coming full circle, returning to my roots with the goal of inspiring and motivating the graduating class. I vividly remembered the dual feelings of my own graduation day: the joy of accomplishment and completion — that sense of knowing I had *arrived* — and the excited, hopeful anticipation of the future.

For these young healthcare professionals, the day marked the closing of one important chapter in their lives and was a gateway to many new opportunities. I encouraged them to embrace the future with enthusiasm and optimism, to be catalysts and change agents, and to use their unique expertise to make a difference. I called on them to be our next generation of leaders, impressing on them my belief that leadership isn't limited to or solely defined by the specific role, rank, position, or title that we may hold. Leadership is a mindset, an ethos, a heartfelt way of relating, interacting, and influencing. It's a way of being.

The graduation speech was a turning point for me, marking a professional reemergence after a two-year hiatus. Preparing for the speech had been an opportunity to mentally revisit and reflect on life since my own graduation. The speech served as a mirror, and my own words of advice and encouragement bounced right back to me. It occurred to me that over the course of our lives, we *arrive* and *commence* again and again, and in the process, we're given the opportunity to stretch and expand, often experiencing progressively deeper levels of understanding and insight with each recursive cycle.

Like the graduates, I, too, was facing a new beginning and ready to reclaim the excitement and hopefulness of the future. A future that was now focused on helping other leaders reach their full potential for the benefit of the communities they served. After 25 years of experience leading at all levels of a large and complex organization, I knew I had more to share and contribute. Writing a short speech about leadership prompted me to begin the process of writing a book about leadership, something I'd been considering for a long time.

But as I started collating and organizing nearly three decades' worth of perspectives and lessons learned, I quickly realized that it would be impossible for me to write authentically without writing about a workplace trauma that had occurred eight years before. As the book began to take shape, I knew that the story of that trauma — a shattering, life-changing event that I had rarely spoken about publicly — would have to be the focal point. Its impact on the organization and influence on my philosophies of leadership could not be denied or disregarded. It had disrupted my existential framework and forced me to question the essence and meaning of life. The trauma — with its wide reach and ceaseless, rippling wake — had altered and transformed me.

The book about leadership naturally evolved into memoir, revealing my experience as a leader with PTSD, and, as a patient with PTSD. Prior to the trauma, I thought I knew what it was like to be a patient. After all, I knew the operations of hospitals and healthcare systems inside and out. I'd undergone minor surgeries, given birth to two babies, and had helped family members and friends navigate through numerous health scares and end-of-life situations. And as a hospital administrator, I'd often been a "secret shopper" to ensure that I remained in touch and empathetic to the patient experience.

But I had never felt as fragile and exposed until I was a patient with PTSD. A patient with a diagnosis that carried stigma and judgment and was often misunderstood, even by the well-meaning people around me. And certainly, by society at large. I learned directly and intimately what it really felt like to be truly vulnerable and at the mercy of the healthcare system. I came to fully understand the axiom "people don't care what you know, until they know that you care." And what I learned as a patient, changed me as a leader.

And though the reasons for writing this book were clear to me, another purpose emerged as I began writing the initial chapters. Eight years later, I was still holding on to the trauma — and it was still holding on to me. Two members of my team had lost their lives, killed in the line of duty. On my watch. And it had been my long-held, firmly entrenched conviction that as the leader during the traumatic event, I was the guardian of that organizational memory. I believed it was my responsibility to remember — to not let go, to never forget.

I was reminded of the wise words of Hermann Hesse: "Some of us think holding on makes us strong; but sometimes it is letting go." I realized that by sharing this story, I could preserve the memory of my colleagues, while letting go of the trauma. Finally, the end of the trauma's long arc was in sight.

Prologue
At the Nadir

I T WAS NEARLY SUNRISE ON MY THIRD DAY at Ridgeview, a place I'd gone to voluntarily, earnestly expecting refuge and asylum. Asylum from my own tormented mind, and refuge from the nearly constant barrage of reports of gun violence — *"BREAKING NEWS"* which never failed to evoke disturbing and debilitating flashbacks, and instantly catapulted me into an endless feedback loop of trauma and terror. And into a state where the past and present blurred. It was impossible to hold back the intrusive flood of emotions and images that always followed. But how could I expect to shut out what was essentially embodied within me? And after years of an incessant cycle of grief and guilt and shame and fear, I had reached my lowest point and was consumed by an overwhelming need to escape, to disappear, to make it all go away.

I had come here desperate for relief and sanctuary, believing it was my only hope for healing and restoration. For redemption. So far, I'd found none of these. Instead, I confronted a rising sense of panic and despair at the realization that perhaps I had even further to fall. I glimpsed new depths of the abyss, made visible in this unexpectedly surreal environment.

Five hundred miles from home, disconnected from everyone I knew, out in the middle of nowhere. I had no way to consistently or privately talk to anyone from home. I no longer had access to music, the Internet, or the outside world. The irony of seeking isolation as a treatment for the damage caused by years of isolation, was not lost on me.

Every two hours I was startled awake by an attendant who barged into my unlocked room at night, scanning and piercing the dark with a bright flashlight. "It's to ensure your safety," I was informed when I complained and questioned the practice for a patient like me. I was agitated, exhausted, irritable, and on-guard. My head ached, and my stomach churned. I felt dizzy and groggy from lack of sleep and being over-medicated. Without a watch or a clock, my disorientation increased. My mind whirled around the words "now here" and their conjugated twin, "nowhere." Now here, nowhere, now here, nowhere...

Worse yet, it seemed that no one here knew *why* I was here. Turned out it was a one-size-fits-all kind of place, despite emphatic assurance prior to my admission that "the program" would be tailored to address my unique needs. I felt angry at being deceived and embarrassed by my gullibility and naïveté.

"Trust the process," I was told repeatedly.

I couldn't help feeling it was a directive, and not an invitation.

I reminded myself that I'd come here on my own and that I could leave anytime I wanted to. I said this again and again. But repeating it didn't convince me it was realistic or true. Leaving didn't seem like an option and I didn't know how to get out without making things worse. I felt powerless. It occurred to me then that I was ostensibly incarcerated, not literally, but rather, in the prison of my own mind. "How did I get here?" I wondered, on the edge of bewilderment. "How did I fall so far that coming here felt like my only option, my last resort?"

My questions began to shift as I second-guessed my strong desire to leave.

"Might it actually be best for me to stay?" I silently asked myself. Maybe experiencing powerlessness and lack of control here would teach me something about myself. Maybe it would help me find my "voice."

I continued mentally probing, scrambling for a rationale, searching for a hidden purpose that could explain my predicament.

"Or maybe it's to confront my own judgments about my disorder?" I paused on the word, *disorder*. And then digressed: was it a condition, an illness, or an injury? I still didn't really know how to accurately name what I was suffering from.

I continued digging and mining for a deeper reason. Maybe I was here to discover what it's truly like to be a vulnerable patient. And to honestly confront the judgment I felt toward the other patients, and, in turn, toward myself.

"Or is it simpler? Will being here make me finally *Get Over It?*" I paused again on this last question, blushing at its harshness.

After a while I was drawn back to the view of the emerging dawn, the desert landscape visible through a large picture window adjacent to my bed. It was a still and silent early winter morning. Deep-purple-onyx mountains formed the lower frame of a glowing horizon. An Ocotillo-Palo Verde-Saguaro trio was silhouetted in sharp relief against the brightening sky. The evolving colors were intense and vivid in the cold, crystal-clear atmosphere. I hated being in this place, but the view was mesmerizing, beautiful, hypnotic. I didn't want to leave yet.

I asked one more question as the sun began to peak above the ridgeline. "Is full surrender the only path to transformation?" I suspected that daylight would bring new awareness, a new awakening. And, yes, of course I thought of Kafka, and hoped that, unlike Gregor, I wouldn't awaken as a bug. I hoped for a butterfly.

***

To understand how I'd gotten here, let me go back to April 16, 2009...

PART

1

4/16

1 Morning Rounds

"I'VE GOT THIS."

With relief and appreciation, and a bit of wonder, I whispered these three words to myself. Just a few minutes before, I'd arrived at work and bounded enthusiastically toward the pedestrian bridge that connected the multi-level parking structure to the main hospital. I paused alone at the top of the walkway to watch the sun as it peaked over the seven-story patient tower. The entire campus was illuminated in golden tones. Already the day was bright and sparkling, but with the gentle coolness of an early spring morning in southern California.

As I took it all in, I repeated the three words aloud for reassurance, as confirmation, and in celebration. I was also crossing a figurative threshold, an important milestone in my early tenure as CEO of Memorial Medical Center. My first 100 days. I felt myself relax as I began to fully comprehend what it would take to be successful in my new role. Though encouraged by my growing confidence, I didn't doubt that I would be frequently tested and challenged in the years to come. Growth, I'd learned, was iterative — often achieved by stretching to the edge and expanding beyond previous limitations. But sometimes it was attained by pausing, contracting, or course-correcting. Wisdom, I would discover, was knowing which was called for.

I couldn't know then that Thursday, the 16th of April 2009 would also become associated with an entirely different Rubicon that marked a definitive "before" and "after" — not just in my career, but in my life and the lives of many others. A day after which I'd never be the same. A day that would forever change me.

***

For more than a century, Memorial had served the diverse, densely populated community of greater Long Beach, California. Home to two large, not-for-profit teaching hospitals — one catering to the healthcare needs of adults and the other to the unique needs of children — the 54-acre campus was one of the biggest and busiest medical center complexes on the West Coast. With nearly $1 billion in annual revenues, more than 6,000 employees, and 1,500 independent physicians and specialists, the hospitals were a major economic engine in a region with a population of more than a million people. Words like "legacy" and "cornerstone" and "premiere" described it. Open 24/7, never closed, it was a city within a city.

From a career perspective, I had grown up in the organization. More than 20 years before, I had arrived as an eager pharmacy student, hoping to secure a permanent position. And when I did, I was hooked. I'd known then that I intended to spend my entire career in this organization. I became part of a tribe, a team of people dedicated to caring for others across the entire spectrum of their lives, literally from birth to death. We welcomed new life. We treated, healed, and saved lives. And we eased lives as they faded and passed. We were a community of caregivers who were there for people on the best days of their lives — and, on their worst, most difficult days. We were a safe haven, a sanctuary for patients coming to us with illnesses and injuries from the outside world. I was professionally "home," and my attachment to it was both rooted in belonging and anchored to purpose and duty.

Over the years, I was promoted to progressively challenging leadership positions, first within my home department of Pharmacy, and later throughout our entire healthcare system. I'd worked at every hospital within the system and at our corporate headquarters, and each new assignment further developed my skills and broadened my experience as a leader. By the time I was appointed CEO of the Long Beach hospitals in early 2009, I had served at nearly every level of the organization and had a deep and thorough understanding of a hospital's inner workings and strategic tactics.

But the responsibilities of this new assignment felt vastly and significantly different than my previous ones. My professional calling was now a covenant to guide, protect, and steward an entire organization. "Ministerial" was the word that came readily to mind. And because I'd previously thought of myself as religiously indifferent, the word caught me by surprise. I privately savored my newfound reverence and felt uplifted and invigorated. Joyful. "I'm *responsible*," I thought to myself, "for my tribe."

***

One of my favorite administrative activities was doing "Rounds" which consisted of wandering the grounds to greet visitors and patients and providing directions around our large campus. I'd also assess the physical surroundings and condition of the facility and inspect the common areas and the lobby. I felt proud to do my little part to make the place orderly and tidy, warm and welcoming. I frequently stopped to chat with employees and doctors to informally survey the temperament of the organization. And while people would often relay concerns and issues, they'd also share good news and successes. We'd often laugh and trade stories about our kids and vacations. I loved this part of my job — and relished being part of a community and tangibly part of something much larger than myself.

I didn't have any meetings scheduled on the morning of April 16th, so my rounds that day were unrushed and extended, which allowed me the opportunity to talk with a lot of staff members. We were in the midst of a difficult budget season which, combined with the financial crash of '08, contributed to an atmosphere of stress and worry that had hung over the organization — and the entire community — for the past several months. Threats of layoffs and cutbacks have a way a dampening the spirit of a workplace. But I was relieved by newly released reports from our finance department indicating that our bottom line had improved substantially. Based on the most-recent results and new projections, we were cautiously optimistic that we could reach our budget targets by June 30th, which was our fiscal year-end.

On my rounds that day, I sensed an overall lightheartedness in the air, an easing up, which replaced the previous pall of anxiety and insecurity. Perhaps this hinted at a return to normalcy and stability, I thought. Or perhaps I was just projecting my own, newly buoyant, increasingly optimistic mood. I would come to realize that I still had a lot to learn about listening fully, with objective curiosity and a willingness to tune-in to legitimate concerns and uncomfortable truths, and not just listening for what I wanted to hear.

Late in the morning, I returned to my office on the ground floor of our hospital tower. My office was adjacent to the main lobby and in a large suite that housed most of the senior executives and the medical staff leaders. At a quarter to noon I left my office and headed to my first scheduled meeting of the day. I was just a few steps out my door when I saw and heard an unusual commotion at the far end of the office suite. A colleague came rushing up to me and grabbed me with uncharacteristic concern and alarm. And unconcealed fear.

"Someone has a gun in the lobby!" she said. Both of us were veterans of crises large and small, but I knew by the tone of her voice that this situation was different, and potentially more terrifying, than anything she and I had ever encountered before.

"Oh, FUCK!" was my initial response.

"Call 911. Call Code Silver. Call the Communications department," I added. My directive came automatically and concisely, as I quickly transitioned into "Incident Command" mode. But the "Oh, Fuck!" betrayed the depth of my concern.

I knew it was critical to alert my boss, whose office was located at our corporate headquarters nearly 20 miles away. Since I'd been scheduled to leave after my noon meeting to attend a conference in San Diego, it was important for her to know that I was still on site and in charge. I rushed back into my office to phone her. The call went through immediately, and I quickly and unemotionally conveyed what little I knew. She was calm and reassuring. I told her I'd call again when I could, and I let her know that I didn't think it was necessary for her to come to Long Beach.

There wasn't anything more for me to say to her, and there wasn't anything she could do from there, so we hung up. But I held the dead receiver for a few moments longer, disquieted by the dull, but grating, dial tone that signaled our disconnection. I couldn't imagine how she'd be able to effectively resume her regularly scheduled day, now that she'd been given this limited, but distressing information. I'd left her with the discomfort of having to blindly wait and wonder from afar. Hanging up had left me feeling strangely alone. No, not alone. Lonely. As in "lonely at the top."

Typically, the next step was to officially call an "Internal Code Triage" to initiate the Hospital Incident Command System — the formal, military-esque system we had in place to manage unplanned emergencies. During a crisis, it was important to establish a clear chain of command and a well-coordinated tactical response. An "Internal" event was one occurring on the medical center grounds — a widespread utility outage, large-scale equipment or computer failure, robberies, suspicious packages, or flooding, for example. An off-campus event that required emergency readiness for a potential influx of mass casualties, like earthquakes, train derailments, or plane crashes, were designated "External." Over the years we had experienced them all and we had drilled for every other disaster scenario we thought possible. But in 2009, an "active shooter" event occurring at a hospital wasn't yet imagined.

Before we could safely call the code, we needed more information because our default Incident Command Center happened to be in the Doctor's Dining Room which was directly upstairs and far too close to the lobby, the apparent epicenter of the crisis. It wasn't safe to summon our department and medical staff leaders, knowing they'd be rushing from all corners of the hospital through a potentially dangerous scene.

From my office, I hurried to the back entrance of the office suite to ensure that we were officially in "Lockdown" and to listen, hoping to get more information about what was happening. The doorway was less than 20 steps from the lobby. With my back to the closed door, I faced a half dozen or so other people; most were physicians who'd descended from the Doctors' Dining Room in response to the commotion. Word had spread quickly that we had an issue.

One doctor asked if we should open the door and go out to the lobby. I answered with a definitive and surprisingly stern, "No." It wasn't a suggestion. I was adamant that no one was to leave the area. Instinctively, I created a physical barrier, throwing my arms across the doorway to block the exit — like I remembered my mother doing when I was a small child riding in the passenger seat of the car, whenever she had to suddenly brake hard to avoid a collision.

It was then that I heard sounds of terror that would haunt me for years. The screams and shrieks were sharp, shrill, harsh and penetrating. They echoed and reverberated discordantly in the vaulted acoustics of the lobby. And as though inexplicably assuming form, the sound travelled down the hallway to the door we were huddled behind. We looked at one another, wide-eyed and frozen. I held my breath.

The screams instantly evoked fear — a primal fear that came involuntarily, as if an existential warning had reflexively erupted from the deep, ancestral recesses of the brain. I didn't need to cognitively process the meaning of the screams. I didn't need to decipher or interpret their message. I didn't need to translate them into words. I didn't need any additional information to know that we were in immense danger.

No one asked again to go to the lobby. We all knew it wasn't safe. Instead we were forced to stay and wait and listen, unable to help. The jagged, piercing screams continued relentlessly. It felt as though our sacred place was being ripped and torn apart.

***

Amidst the din, but still behind the closed door, I silently pleaded and begged, repeating the word, *"please,"* — mantra-like — as though it would will away any potential harm.

"Please, please, please, please, please..."

I began conjuring up explanations that could account for both the initial report of a gun in the lobby and the horrific screaming — and still result in an acceptable outcome. One in which everyone was safe and unhurt.

The potential scenarios spanned a broad spectrum of escalating danger, stopping short of catastrophe, while still clinging to optimism:

- It's just a terrible prank with a fake or toy gun...
- It's someone threatening, but with an unloaded gun...
- It's a threat with a real gun, but it will be de-escalated before someone gets hurt...
- It's a robbery, but the robber will get away — and no one will chase after the robber or try to be a hero...
- If someone does get hurt, it won't be a serious injury...

My attempts to convince myself that it would all be okay were interrupted by an eerie silence. The screams had stopped but the interlude was brief, lasting, what felt like just a few long seconds.

The sounds that resumed were distinctly different — dissonant screams of fear were replaced with synchronized cries of agony — a collective wailing of grief that was gut-wrenching and heartbreaking. Even now, I struggle to adequately describe the sounds and the acute suffering they conveyed.

These new sounds carried much more meaning than the previous ones. No longer were they signals of foreboding or warnings of things to come. They were now reports, informing me of what was undeniably horrendous news. All the wishful thinking, the "Please, God" bargaining, and the hopes that, maybe, just maybe, nothing bad *would* happen, were dashed. I knew then that something bad *had* happened; something awful enough to produce abject sounds of pain and anguish.

Earlier my mind and body had braced against the incoming, external sounds of terror; now, the clenching served instead to steady me against my own emotions. I felt an unfamiliar tingling in my face and jaw, and a heaviness in my limbs. And an oddly warm and tightening sensation in my chest, as though my heart were simultaneously squeezing and exploding. I felt a rising panic that the panic, itself, might consume me. Over the previous 20 years, I had faced dozens of extremely difficult and stressful situations. None had evoked this type of emotion, this degree of fear.

And then an entirely new sound emerged from the hallway. The heavy thudding, intense pounding, and thundering of boots. The sound roared down the hall like a freight train and charged toward the lobby. The police had arrived.

I rushed back to my office to call my boss a second time. Though I didn't have many new facts to share, I could now report that it was a serious and, likely, calamitous situation. My voice was surprisingly calm as I updated her. But the real reason for calling her was to request her help. While I expected that the police would take charge of the initial tactical response, I knew I'd need a different kind of help as the event evolved and extended into an aftermath that I would be responsible for leading us through.

"I need you come to Long Beach, right now, right away," I insisted, without reservation or hesitation.

"I need you for emotional support," I added, without any embarrassment about the disclosure. Despite having led through many crises over the years, I had never said those words before. I'd never needed to.

I raced back to the closed door. I'd dressed more casually than usual in anticipation of the conference I'd planned to attend later in the day, in pants instead of a skirt, and in flats instead of heels, so I didn't have to jog on my toes back to the door. I sprinted all-out. The running was jarring and forced me to breathe heavily and more evenly. The oxygen helped to keep me focused on the job before me — leading in what I now knew was a full-blown crisis. From that moment on, and at least for the next several years, focusing and re-focusing on the job at hand kept my feelings at bay. Mostly.

***

When facing a crisis, I'd been trained to first think broadly and expansively, to identify all the possible scenarios, and then to systematically and rationally zero in on those most likely, in a process of elimination as new information emerged. I would also force myself to imagine the worst thing that was logically and rationally possible. Not because I pessimistically expected the worst, but as a strategy to psychologically navigate potential fear, panic, and anxiety in advance. Paradoxically, by pre-empting shock and minimizing surprise, this form of "inverse thinking" had a calming and steadying effect. It allowed me to compose myself and compartmentalize my emotions during a crisis, making room for and creating the space to solve problems with sharper clarity and focus. I now admit, it was a method rooted also in a bit of superstition: if I imagined the worst, then magically, "the worst" wouldn't or couldn't happen. And after all, it never had.

But my list of all imagined possibilities had to now include someone being gravely wounded or dead. Based on what I knew, I narrowed it to what I thought was most likely:

- The gift shop or the outpatient pharmacy had been robbed (both were in the lobby), and someone had been hurt in the process, or
- It was violence involving a gang or gangs (prior to then, the hospital had been respected as a neutral zone), or
- A patient or family member had hurt a staff member, or
- A fight between visitors had become violent, or
- A fight had occurred involving an employee and their significant other.

That was about the extent of my list. It didn't end up being any of these. Turned out, I hadn't identified all the worst-case possibilities. I hadn't been capable of imagining them.

The thundering boots had stopped but the commotion in the lobby continued, and now other noises joined the agonizing keening and wailing. I heard an overhead page for "Code Blue" and then the loud, commanding voice of a policeman. I opened the door, peered out into the hallway, and saw an officer I recognized. He signaled that the immediate danger had passed.

The keening and wailing continued relentlessly. The sounds repelled and, simultaneously, pulled at me like a magnet, forcing me to make a choice: I could go upstairs to the Incident Command Center and await further instruction from the police, or I could go out to the lobby to be with, and directly help, people who I knew were in serious distress. It would be understandable and explainable if I'd chosen the former; after all, it would be expected in any other event. Although I had a clinical background, as an administrator, my first-response duty was usually reserved for serving as Incident Commander, rather than providing direct patient care. But this wasn't like any other event. I knew I'd never forgive myself if I chose to go upstairs, avoiding and retreating, secretly using my conventional role of Incident Commander as an excuse, as cover, for my fear.

I knew in my heart that going out to the lobby was what was most needed, what was called for. But it was a fateful decision. While I believed I wasn't putting myself in physical danger, I never considered the possibility of psychic shattering. Courage, I would learn, was as much about the actions you took in the face of fear, as it was about bearing witness to what unfolded as a result.

————◆————

"Reality is what we take to be true. What we take to be true is what we believe. What we believe is based upon our perceptions. What we perceive depends on what we look for. What we look for depends on what we think. What we think depends on what we perceive. What we perceive determines what we believe. What we believe determines what we take to be true. What we take to be true is our reality."

~ David Bohm, Physicist

————◆————

Into the Void

WITH AN "ALL CLEAR" SIGN FROM THE POLICEMAN in the hallway, I stepped out into the corridor and ran toward the screaming. It was coming from the Outpatient Pharmacy, which was located at the far end of the lobby, near the main entrance of the hospital. When I reached the foyer of the pharmacy, I saw a group of first responders attending a man who was stretched out on the ground, lying flat on his back. He was dressed in business clothes, in a shirt and tie, but jacketless, the soles of his shoes facing my direction. I didn't know who he was, and I couldn't tell if he was a staff member or a visitor. The gunshot wounds to his head and face made him unrecognizable. But I had no doubt at all that he was dead.

I had always been amazed at the way code blue teams sprang into action — and awed by how their seamless and fluid choreography brought coherence and control to chaos. I admired the team members' tenacity and resolve and was inspired by their eternal hopefulness and determination to overcome all odds to save lives and to prevent death. But it was heartbreaking that day to watch their futile efforts.

The scene unfolded in silent slow motion, as if my brain were trying to catch up, trying to comprehend what I was seeing and hearing. It was the first of several dissociative gaps in perception and reality that I experienced that day.

I soon became aware of screaming that was louder than the rest. It blared and beckoned, refusing to be ignored. The screams were coming from a woman who was standing about 10 feet from the man on the ground. I recognized her as one of the pharmacy technicians who worked in the Outpatient Pharmacy. She was sobbing hysterically. She appeared physically uninjured but was obviously in severe emotional pain and needed help. I ran to her.

She saw me approaching and I saw the look of recognition on her face. She reached frantically out for me and then gripped my hands tightly, holding on as though she never intended to let go, like the way a drowning person desperately grabs a life preserver. And then, as if no one else existed, we slumped to the floor, first to our knees, and then all the way down, facing one another.

What happened next remains one of the most astonishing and unexplainable experiences in my life. Wide, jagged streaks of blinding white light flared out wildly from her body, forming an aura around her head and upper torso. It was as if her emotions were bursting out — too heated, too extreme, too overwhelming — to be contained. But even more shocking and confusing was that the light seemed to be cracking her in half, right down the middle.

I was either witnessing something I'd previously thought impossible, or I was hallucinating. Was she having a psychotic break? I wondered if looking away would make the image disappear. It didn't.

And although I was suddenly frightened by her, I was more afraid *for* her. I wanted to comfort her, but I felt inept and incapable; I couldn't think of anything to say that I thought could possibly help. It seemed the only way to help was to hold on to her, to not let go.

She stared at me with intensity and pulled at me with urgency, as though she needed to tell me something important. Struggling to hear her words, I leaned in more closely.

"How could you let this happen?" she said with an angry, indignant tone that completely surprised me.

"How could *you* let this happen?" she repeated, as though I hadn't heard her the first time. The emphasis on *you* made it clear she meant me, personally.

"Diana, you had to know that this would happen!" I was stunned, caught off-guard by the accusation. And confused.

Why would she be blaming me? What did she mean by what she'd said? My mind scrambled for answers, for clues. I tried to get her to say more, to clarify what she meant, but she just repeated "you *knew* that this would happen" and "Diana, how could you let this happen?" again and again. The words stung. I rolodexed through all the scenarios I had previously envisioned, telling myself that she couldn't possibly be implicating me personally. She must have meant "The Hospital" in place of "You." People did that all the time...I'd begun to grow used to it.

But I couldn't shake how different it felt this time. I couldn't deny how personal the accusation felt. Given what I knew so far, I couldn't yet make sense of what she had said. I couldn't think of anything that I had done, or not done, that could have caused, or would have prevented a man from being shot and killed in the

Outpatient Pharmacy. But her insistence on my culpability was alarming. A red flag. A warning.

The accusation had touched an undefended nerve, evoking a feeling of blame that I had not anticipated. A warm prickling sensation began to spread across my face and neck and down my arms to my hands. Defensiveness bubbled to the surface of my mind.

I soon became aware, though, of the other people around us who were gathered in small groups, hugging one another, crying and weeping, grief-stricken. The man on the ground had been identified as Hugo, the supervisor of the Outpatient Pharmacy. I looked to see the reaction on the pharmacy technician's face. But, of course, she already knew who he was. She had witnessed her boss being brutally murdered. And I began to better understand just how deeply she had been wounded.

***

"Mario ran down the hallway," she suddenly and anxiously blurted out. She seemed concerned primarily for his well-being, as if she wished she'd been able to stop him from leaving the pharmacy. Her voice was barely a whisper, and her words trailed off, as though she were talking to herself and not to me at all. It alarmed me to hear that Mario, who was also a pharmacy technician, had gone running after the shooter. Everyone knew you shouldn't do that. It had been drilled into us all to never approach a person who had a weapon. If you heard "Code Silver," you sheltered in place until the situation was resolved by security or law enforcement. I worried that he had foolishly put himself at risk by chasing an armed and obviously dangerous person.

Known by almost everyone in the hospital as one of the friendliest and most outgoing employees, Mario was usually the first person encountered at the Outpatient Pharmacy. He had a reputation for being jovial and outgoing, often personally delivering employees' prescriptions to their units or departments so that they wouldn't have to wait in line at the busy pharmacy during their breaks or lunch time.

He had been recently honored at our "Applause Awards" luncheon, a quarterly event that recognized employees for their exceptional service. The ceremony was an important part of our history and culture, an opportunity for us to celebrate the special and remarkable work done by our staff members. Nominations from coworkers, doctors, patients, and family members were often sentimental, heartfelt, and emotionally moving, and were traditionally read aloud at the luncheon for all to hear. Rarely was there a dry eye in the room.

When Mario was honored, his two bosses, Hugo and Kelly, shared letters from patients and coworkers highlighting his extraordinary teamwork and helpfulness. He was effusively described as frequently going "above and beyond" and always willing to extend an extra effort to help others. Everyone in the room talked about his sense of humor and how he'd crack jokes everywhere he went, bringing welcome laughter to an often-serious workplace. All the reports were unanimously glowing. But to me they were confusing — because my perception of Mario had been completely different.

I seemed to be the only person who was puzzled by the gushing praise of him. When I arrived at the awards ceremony, I was genuinely shocked to discover that he'd been nominated, and equally surprised that he had been selected as an honoree. Though I had never worked directly with him, I saw him once a month when I stopped by the Outpatient Pharmacy to pick up a prescription for one of my family members. In my experience, Mario was brooding and glowering and conveyed an over-the-top deference toward me that seemed feigned and disingenuous. On the surface he was polite and courteous, but it felt thinly veiled, begrudging, almost mocking — as though he wasn't trying very hard to hide his disrespect. I assumed that was how he interacted with everyone else, too.

He must not like his job, I had assumed. Obviously, he had a chip on his shoulder.

But, based on how he was described at the ceremony, I thought that I must have been wrong — that I'd misjudged him. Because, clearly, he was loved by many throughout the entire hospital.

In the few months following the Applause ceremony, I tried harder to get to know him and to repair our uneasy rapport, but nothing reduced the discomfort I felt around him. He often seemed purposely unreachable and unapproachable. His animus toward me was unmistakable, made more noticeable because he was so openly friendly, and even playful, with others. I wondered why he didn't like me but tried not to take it too personally. We'd never had an argument or conflict, so I assumed it was "The Hospital" that he didn't like. Perhaps, I thought, he viewed me as an extension of it because of my role, because of the authority I represented. People did that all the time...I'd begun to grow used to it.

But when I was told that Mario had run down the hallway, presumably chasing after the shooter, I wasn't completely shocked, given what I knew about Mario's high regard for his coworkers and his reputation for reaching out to help others.

"Mario ran after the shooter?" I asked, hopeful that I'd misheard or misunderstood her.

"No," she said, "Mario *is* the shooter."

The revelation that Mario had killed his boss shocked and jolted me to the core. Like a bolt of lightning. Despite my history with him, I had not seen that coming. But I now had an inkling into why she'd said, "You should have known this would happen." I had leaned in to help her and exposed myself to a form of danger I had not expected or imagined.

I recoiled, trying to pull away to get some distance from her, but she latched onto me even more tightly, and I was momentarily frozen, held captive by the intensity of her stare and her iron grip. But I was also held captive by the force of my own mind, which scrambled to deny her accusation, while already beginning to believe there might be some truth to it.

***

Though stunned, the news that the shooter was an insider propelled me to act. The woman I was with needed professional help, and I needed to get out of the pharmacy. I called out to a nearby group for assistance, and, once I knew she was in good hands, with people who could care for her, I ran toward a policeman standing in the main lobby. I noticed that almost everyone else had been evacuated.

The officer told me that instead of going out the nearby front doors of the hospital, Mario had gone in the opposite direction, down the long hallway that connected the main hospital to the Emergency Department, the "ED," and had then exited the building. And that he was dead. His body, he said, was on the street just outside. The officer also told me that a joint Hospital/Police Department Incident Command Center would be established on the north side of the hospital, in that same general vicinity.

"It's a murder/suicide," the officer informed me. He appeared unfazed, almost stoic.

"It's over, ma'am," he told me, his tone firm and confident, as though to convince me, to assure me, of its finality.

It was no longer an "active shooter" situation, he explained. And then I understood the reason for his calm steadiness. There was no longer anyone to apprehend or to protect. The shooter was dead. The threat was now neutralized, the scene secured, the event contained. For him, it was over. For many of the rest of us, it was going to be a long way to "over."

After many conversations over the years with law enforcement and other first responders, I realize now that interpreting his demeanor as evidence that, for him, it was "over," was probably inaccurate and incomplete, if not also outrightly unfair. More than likely, the officer would carry the images of this scene — and countless others like it — for the rest of his life. He'd likely wrestle with the secondary stress of frequent exposure to violent death. He'd likely handle it, manage it, and adapt to it in healthy ways, but each event would remain with him, regardless of his outward stoicism and the strength he conveyed. As I recall his words all these years later, I still hear the confidence and assurance in his tone. But now I hear the relief in his voice too. Relief, that he could report that the violence was over, even if its effects were not.

As my conversation with the police officer was ending, I saw that Hugo's body was now on a gurney and was being taken down the long hallway towards the Emergency Department. From there, the staff would notify his family.

Oh!

I suddenly realized that we couldn't default to our usual protocols for notifying a trauma patient's next of kin. *This was our own employee. He had been killed here, in his place of work. By another employee. By an employee in his department. By an employee he supervised. By a fellow team member. In the hospital.* We'd lived in a bubble of safety and sanctuary. We cared for people who had been injured — out there. We saved people from what happened — out there. I had believed that it couldn't happen — in here.

Our routine procedures for contacting patients' loved ones seemed far too callous and inadequate for these extraordinary circumstances. We needed to think this through. *Who should call Hugo's wife to tell her? What if she were alone? Should someone drive over to her and escort her back? Who had her phone number? Should I run down to Human Resources to retrieve it? How could we possibly soften the blow for her?*

And then I caught myself, struck by the realization that I knew her name, that I knew about her and their family from a conversation I'd recently had with Hugo. He had been so proud of them. I remembered that his face lit up when he talked about his kids and how important it had been for him to be fully present, fully engaged with them...after all, he'd said, they grow up so quickly. I struggled to contain my emotions and fought to clear my head. The simplest problem to solve — the logistics of getting a phone number — suddenly seemed so complicated and complex. I had been knocked off-balance by what I'd seen and heard. I was not accustomed to feeling bewildered and indecisive. Everything was foggy and hazy. My thinking felt frustratingly slow and sluggish.

My highest priority was making sure that we connected with Hugo's wife in the most compassionate, sensitive way possible. I thought then of Hugo's boss, Kelly — he would know Hugo's wife and could be there for her as she was told. That moment of clarity — reconnecting with my own agency and the overwhelming need to do something — momentarily snapped me out of confusion and propelled me into action.

I ran to catch up and to intervene.

* * *

The door to the back entrance of the ED was propped open and I saw that a lot of people were spilled out into the hallway. A flurry of activity was coming from inside the trauma room, where, surrounding a man on a gurney, a medical response team worked to save his life. I silently entered the room and stood a few feet away, searching for clues to his identity. I knew it wasn't Hugo or Mario, but at first, I didn't recognize the patient.

I don't know if it was because of the extensive damage to the man's face or because I was unable to comprehend that there was *another* victim in the shooting. As I'd run to the ED, it had never occurred to me that more than one person had been shot by Mario. In the Lobby outside the Outpatient Pharmacy, the officer had said "murder-suicide." It dawned on me that "murder-suicide" was a descriptive label, a category, and wasn't meant to indicate extent or quantity.

No one ever said, "murders-suicide."

I noticed the man's right arm was dangling off the gurney and my eyes traced the path from bare shoulder to bicep, down his freckled arm to his hand, and lastly, to his fingers, which were outstretched in the space between us. On his ring finger was a distinctive signet ring that I recognized immediately. It belonged to my colleague and dear friend of more than 20 years. The patient was Hugo's boss, Kelly. I gasped in surprise and grabbed the med cart to steady myself. I'd been hit by an emotional two-by-four.

What was Kelly doing in here?! He can't be in here! Why was he on the gurney?! Why isn't he moving?! My mind was flooded with confusion and denial, posed as questions. Refusing to accept that Kelly had been shot, I rushed to his side and irrationally waved my arms, motioning wildly for him to get up.

"Kelly, you need to get off the gurney, you're in the way!" I demanded, as though my insistence that he move out of the way could reverse what had happened to him. That it could somehow make it untrue.

And then my mind finally caught up to the reality of what I had experienced — fully absorbing the sounds of terror, the gruesome images, the emotions of raw fear and suspense, the feeling of extreme surprise. And the accusation that I was to blame. I'd been propelled over the edge of an abyss I hadn't known existed and cast into a liminal void of ambiguity, confusion, and dissociation. I struggled to regain equilibrium as I felt myself unraveling. My body began to shake, my heart pounded, my breathing was rapid and shallow, my vision blurry. Inside, I screamed *"NO, NO, NO, NO, NO, NO, NO, NO, NO, NO, NO, NO, NO, NO, NO, NO, NO, NO..."*

Now I was the one beginning to crack open. But initially, the gap wasn't where the light would shine in; it was where the newly planted seeds of guilt and culpability would grow. Silently, invisibly, persistently.

And simultaneously, as the responsible leader, and the leader responsible, an irrepressible sense of duty emerged — the duty to close the gap and to seal the wound — which bonded me even more tightly to the organization. "The Hospital" and I were now inseparable, fused by *responsibility.*

***

The Trauma Room was now quiet and nearly empty. Though it felt like an eternity, less than 30 minutes had passed since I had been told there was a gun in the lobby. I could still hear screaming, but the sounds I now heard were entirely within me, completely contained and confined inside. Outwardly, I was silent. Kelly lay motionless on the gurney. Discarded packaging materials, supply wrappers, and empty vials littered the light green tile floor below him. Red lights on the monitoring equipment flashed and pulsed, silently demanding attention. And though I was vaguely aware of a couple of figures standing still and ghost-like in the background, Kelly and I were alone in the room. Only later did that seem implausible or inaccurate, or an artifact of my memory. Because, of course Kelly would not have been left unattended by the trauma response team.

He was still alive.

My perceptions of time and space were temporarily warped and altered. Spell-bound in an intense and desperate fight for life, I believed I *was* alone with Kelly in that room, cohabitating an other-worldly space between life and death. He desperately clung to life — and I desperately clung to him. In this mystical dimension, I reached out to hold his outstretched hand. I didn't want him to feel alone or to suffer. I didn't want him to be afraid or in pain. I didn't want to let him go. I didn't want him to die. I didn't want to lose my kind, gentle friend.

For many years, I revisited this scene again and again, in my sleep and while wide awake, haunted not by the question of whether my perceptions that day had been real or flawed, but by the unshakeable feeling that I was entombed in my own ghostly state. Unresolved and unforgiven, unable to let go of him and unable to hold on to him, I was neither dead, nor entirely alive. It was as if I remained entangled with him at the threshold of our two deaths, though his physical one would come sooner than mine.

"The speed at which we find explanations for things that happen makes it difficult for us to learn the deep truth."

~ *Daniel Kahneman*

"The truth you believe and cling to makes you unavailable to hear anything new."

~ *Pema Chodron*

---

3 Ours, too

NEW ACTIVITY IN THE TRAUMA ROOM snapped me back to real-time awareness; the physician-in-charge informed us that Kelly was being transported to an operating room. The news sparked hope and stoked feelings of purpose and agency. Even though we were in shock, we each had our own roles to fill while the trauma team worked heroically, trying to save the life of one of our own.

As the CEO, I needed to connect with the police commander to understand the entirety of the situation and to launch our team's response. There would be a lot to do. We needed to immediately establish crisis counseling services, conduct a comprehensive assessment, develop a coordinated communication plan, identify gaps and unknowns, and implement our initial action plans. And we still needed to notify Hugo's wife. And now Kelly's wife. And Mario's.

He was ours, too.

I emerged from the trauma room and made my way through the interior corridors of the Emergency Department and out to the north side of the hospital toward the Incident Command Center. Along the way, I encountered people whose faces were streaked with tears, their eyes conveyed confusion and disbelief, their shoulders slumped with the weight of sorrow. We didn't have the words to express our feelings, so we hugged to comfort and soothe, and to uphold one another. Though we were accustomed to being in the presence of grief, this was a kind of grief that was both unspeakable, and impossible to hold alone.

In each embrace, I repeatedly overheard the word *why*, initially uttered in barely audible whimpers, but then growing steadily into a pleading cry.

"*Why?*...

Why?...

Why?...

Why?..."

The question, which is so familiar to anyone in grief, exposed our compulsive, fundamentally human need to know the cause, or have a reason, especially when faced with unexpected tragedy and loss. And, in the search for that answer, it seems nearly impossible to resist the natural impulse to jump to any conclusion that relieves the extreme discomfort of not knowing. Because if we have an answer, we can then *do something* to regain our sense of safety and security, restore order and certainty to our lives, and prevent it from ever happening again. And if, in our rush to judgment, a seemingly logical and plausible answer is quickly offered, the leap from speculation to concretized belief can be instantaneous. Especially if the answer is echoed by a group, reinforcing the belief each time it's repeated.

I would come to appreciate that knowing *why* serves as a powerful antidote to feelings of loss of control and helplessness, and to the fear and apprehension of the unknown. And I would also come to understand that some answers to *why* had the potential to inflict far-reaching and long-lasting harm.

So, while I shared the instinct to ask and answer the question *"why?,"* I bristled each time I heard it asked aloud. I wasn't sure I could bear to know why. I couldn't trust that knowing why would restore my sense of safety and security; likely, it would do the exact opposite. Because I was afraid of the conclusion I suspected I'd hear from others — the one I'd already jumped to myself. I tried to bury the nascent, but growing, dread. I kept moving toward the joint Incident Command Center, which was also in its early stages of formation.

Once at the site, we announced over the PA system and via email that the immediate danger had passed. We asked staff members to stay in their units and to avoid the crime scenes, and said we'd share more information as soon as we could. We were officially on Diversion — meaning that all ambulances and paramedics were re-directed to other hospital Emergency Departments. Police barricades and our own security force surrounded the entire campus.

Over the next hour, I went back and forth between the three crime scenes at least a dozen times to gather additional information and to prepare for broader communication. At each scene, people huddled together in small groups of four or five, consoling one another and sharing what little information they had. It was clear that the full extent of the event was not yet widely known. Information had been slow to spread between the crime scenes, mostly due to the sizeable distance and the restricted-access doorways between them. This was before the widespread use of smartphones and the prevalence of social media. I tried to reassure people that we were now safe and that it was over, catching myself each time I said the word "over," sensing deep down that the effects of the trauma were, in some ways, just beginning.

Though few people were permitted to enter the facility, we still had more than 600 patients in-house and at least a dozen surgeries underway. Including Kelly's. We couldn't completely close down or stop our operations in response to the shooting. We still had patients to care for, even as we managed our own trauma.

Despite exposure to terror and raw emotional pain, the mood at the Incident Command Center was surprisingly calm, and a generous spirit of camaraderie and altruism was palpable. A collective sense of allegiance and purpose served to neutralize much of the chaos, revealing humanity at its best and deepening our connections to one another. It wasn't the first time I'd had a bonding experience with my co-workers in response to disaster, and it wouldn't be the last time that I'd witness our team at its very best. But on that day our better angels were never more visible, ironically in response to a hellish act by one of our own.

On one of my trips between the crime scenes, I was drawn to a small group of people who were gathered just outside the Emergency Department. They were upset that the helicopters, which had begun to circle above, had a clear view of Mario's body. Demands to cover his body to protect his dignity were made repeatedly — a show of deference that seemed disconnected and disproportional to the situation. I was initially annoyed and confused by the request. And angry. He was the murderer, not a victim. But he didn't seem to be viewed that way by all.

Even though the police were adamant that his body was part of a crime scene and could not be touched or moved, the requests that we intervene to cover him continued with increasing agitation. We were momentarily at an impasse. After considerable back-and-forth and handwringing, we came to a workable compromise that both honored the requests and abided by the rules of crime scene preservation: a short time later, a "pop-up" canopy was positioned over his body to obscure the view from the helicopters above.

At the time, I resented bending over backwards and capitulating to what seemed like outlandish demands to protect his dignity. I doubt we would have covered the body of a stranger or an outsider who invaded our hospital and brutally assassinated two of our colleagues. But I later recognized that the act of covering him, ostensibly to protect *his* dignity, actually preserved our own. But in dark moments, I also wondered if covering him up had been a way, figuratively, of concealing our own collective shame.

He was ours, too.

***

A short while later, my boss arrived from the corporate office. It seemed so long ago that I'd called her, and, with all that had happened, I'd forgotten that she was coming. She'd had to park far away and had a tough time getting into the medical center because the campus was on lockdown. She stayed by my side for most of the next several hours, coordinating between various departments and agencies, offering suggestions, intervening where she could, and helping to navigate our response. Her rock-solid and competent demeanor was stabilizing to our operations — and for our emotions. It would have been hard to make it through the rest of the day without her.

A few other senior leaders from the health system and members of our Board of Directors also began to arrive at the hospital and gather at the Incident Command Center. The president of our health system joined soon after as well. Though he and I had known each for a long time, I surprised myself by immediately rushing into his arms as soon as I saw him — I felt a rush of relief and gratefulness that he'd come to the campus.

But I surprised myself again when I deliberately pulled away from him and abruptly ended the hug. And by the look on his face, I thought I'd caught him by surprise, too. It wasn't that I didn't want to keep hugging him — I did — but I'd felt my emotions welling up inside and knew that if I stayed, even a second longer, in a comforting embrace, I'd be unable to hold back an avalanche of tears. And if I started crying, I didn't think I'd be able to stop. Maybe ever. I knew I needed to maintain my composure and to remain focused on everything that needed to be done. I'd cry later, I told myself.

And, in that same split-second, I had another reason to pull away from him: I didn't want to get make-up on his bright white, freshly pressed shirt. It had seemed weird at the time that both reasons for pulling away felt equally compelling to me. Funny how the mind can consider practicalities and manage overwhelming emotions at the same time. I later wondered if he'd thought it was strange that I'd jerked away so suddenly, without explanation. I never did bring it up with him, however, for fear that it would make me cry. And fear that I wouldn't be able to stop. Maybe ever.

A little after two o'clock in the afternoon, I was notified by the Police Department's Public Information Officer and our Communications director that within the next hour, "we," along with the Mayor and Police Chief, would be doing a short, televised press conference. For a moment, I genuinely wondered who would be speaking on our behalf. A second later it dawned on me that, of course, as the CEO, it would need to be me. The "we" was me.

As I began to write the statement, I realized few facts about the crime could be revealed and how little was really known. But I knew it was important to reassure our own organization and the community at large that our patients and the rest of our employees were safe. I imagined how someone on the outside might feel if they'd already heard about the shooting and hadn't been able to connect with a loved one inside. I thought of my own family. I'd not been successful contacting them yet and realized this was likely also the case for thousands of others at the medical center. Though we weren't yet able to name the victims and shooter, I hoped to reduce unnecessary worry and panic by reassuring people on the outside that next of kin had already been notified.

With Mario's body in the background, less than 100 yards away and clearly visible to the small crowd of reporters we faced, the press conference began a little before 3pm. It was a strange coincidence that we were holding it so close to the crime scene, but it was our default location for all press conferences — the tall medical buildings, the Emergency Department, and ambulances provided the quintessential backdrop of a hospital.

By mid-afternoon, the mid-April sun was gleaming and surprisingly intense. A mirage shimmered off the hot asphalt on the closed-off street. I wondered for a moment why we hadn't thought to erect another "pop-up" canopy at the press conference site. Something that would cover us from the glare and reflection.

The Mayor began with a short introductory statement and reported that just before noon a tragedy had occurred at the medical center. After talking about fortitude and resolve and that our community would rally together in response, he turned it over to the Chief of Police, who also acknowledged the valor and bravery of the first responders. There wasn't much more that could be specifically shared. But I cringed when his tone shifted, and he began talking about the phenomenon of active shootings that were "becoming a trend that we've seen nationwide." I stiffened and held my breath when he added, "probably because of the tension that's going on in our society today." He seemed to be hinting at a reason, presumably tying the current recession and the stress of living with financial hardship to the tragedy. I wanted to hear the Chief say that it didn't matter what the reason or cause or the motive was. I wanted to hear him say that the shooter alone was at fault, that he was solely responsible. But he didn't say anything more beyond referring to the current stress in our society.

And then he turned it over to me. I handed my sunglasses to my boss and walked to the podium, squinting into the cameras as I began to read the brief, hand-written statement that I held in my shaking hands:

"It's with a heavy heart that I address you today," I said somberly.

"I'm heartbroken to announce that two members of our employee family have been killed, and another is in critical condition." As I finished the sentence, I was suddenly at a loss, and the words hung in an uncomfortable pause.

Because, in fact, all three were dead. Moments before the start of the press conference, I'd been told that Kelly had died. But I couldn't correct my statement. We were still in the process of updating his family.

I took in a shallow little breath and continued. Throughout the entire event, I said, "our first priority was to ensure the safety of our patients — and that they were well cared for."

"And I can assure you that our patients are safe," I added.

I briefly announced the availability of crisis counseling for our staff and families, but then I abruptly finished. I folded my paper and walked back into the crowd that stood supportively behind me. Questions that we couldn't yet answer were politely, but insistently, shouted at us. We didn't answer any of them but arranged for a Press Q&A in the early evening and told reporters that we'd release more information about the victims, the shooter, and the motive, as soon as possible.

***

While the facts about what had happened were slow to spread across the campus, speculation about *why* it happened, was not. As feared, questions about *why,* turned quickly into whispered answers. The rumor that Mario had been upset about upcoming layoffs circulated around the hospital with dizzying and, to me, sickening, speed. I was stunned to learn that a woman who had been interviewed on TV had echoed the rumor and to hear others referring to Mario as "a great and wonderful man" who had shot his bosses because of fear or anger about layoffs.

In retrospect, *why* was a simple question that would lead to tangled and complicated answers. Initially the question churned up a long list of motives, across a broad range of possible reasons or causes. But it also cast a wide net of secondary blame — blame extending well-beyond the actions of the shooter. Understandably, those closest to the trauma would be caught in a web of guilt and self-blame. Those further from it seemed to find it easier to make sweeping generalizations about the motive. Some held the organization, the recession, or others responsible. Some simply proclaimed that the shooter had been crazy — because only a crazy person would shoot people. Most would be able to assign blame where it did belong, solely with the shooter himself. But some of us would struggle with that.

Though I didn't know every detail of the event, I did know that after killing his supervisor, Mario had left the Outpatient Pharmacy, without hurting or threatening anyone else. He'd run through the lobby, down the long hallway through the busy Radiology Department, and had exited the main hospital. Waving a gun in his hand as he ran, he'd passed many coworkers along the way, calling out to several by name and telling them to get out of the way — because, he'd said, he didn't want to hurt them. On the street outside, he'd then encountered his boss's boss and shot him several times at point-blank range. Afterwards, he'd paced nearby for a few moments before shooting and killing himself, as the police descended on the scene. So, while establishing a motive was premature, what was known was that the shooting wasn't an accident. It wasn't a mishap, or a case of Kelly and Hugo being in the wrong place at the wrong time. It wasn't a random act. It was purposeful and intentional.

To make sense of what had happened, each of us would create a narrative based on our own perspectives and unique histories. And while many motives would be conjured up and considered over the course of the investigation, the one related to layoffs would remain steadfastly and stubbornly lodged in my mind, affixed to my own feelings of guilt. Guilt about the layoff itself, and, guilt for surviving, while my colleagues did not. And knowing it was irrational wouldn't alleviate the guilt or convince me otherwise. Knowing it was misattributed and misdirected would not diminish the guilt I felt. Trauma has a way of injecting guilt into those closest to it, or those most affected by it.

My internal voice of blame would also be bolstered by comments made by others — comments that were insensitive on the one hand, but not entirely surprising to hear on the other. After all, we've probably all overheard comments like these, made in reference to an act of violence:

> "He was so nice, someone or something must have made him do it."

> "He must have had a good reason, otherwise, he never would have done it."

> "You can only push someone so far until they explode."

> "He did it for us, in retaliation for layoffs."

Over the coming days and weeks, it would become apparent to me that others also harbored guilty feelings and self-blame for the roles they, too, believed they'd played in the tragedy. They would search their memories for any clue or evidence of their own culpability, tormenting themselves with the trauma-induced magical thinking that they'd somehow caused it or contributed to it. They would torture themselves by thinking they'd missed a crucial sign — that they should have seen it coming. They would worry that a complaint or a grievance they'd shared with him had somehow provoked or prodded him into action. They would ruminate on all the ways they could have, or should have, stopped it. They would wonder how a person they regarded as a good, trusted friend could do something so awful. They would doubt their own judgment. They would question how he could have been recently honored as an employee-of-the-month. They would be racked with guilt for surviving. And they'd rethink it all again and again.

We would each scramble to find a motive that could offer freedom from implication or recrimination — any motive that would distance ourselves and absolve our guilt. A motive that would relieve feelings of fault — and the immense stress and unbearable pain associated with it. A motive that let us off the hook.

So, in a way, it made sense to me that "layoff-as-motive" would emerge so quickly. It could then be "The Hospital's" fault. "The Hospital" was responsible. After all, no one thought of "The Hospital" as a person...

And once formed, the layoff-as-motive rumor was perseverant, and threatened to become engrained as an organizational urban legend. For me, it was the beginning of a confusing internal debate about motive, and its intertwined relationship to cause and effect. A debate further complicated by my own secretly held shame about the layoff. A layoff that, while justified as a routine, commonly used tool of budget management, had not seemed absolutely necessary at the time.

While I tried to suppress my private anguish about the emerging motive, I was mostly consumed with the realistic fear that it would become a powerfully divisive wedge within the organization, with the potential to irreparably split us in half.

I understood there was the natural urge to unite against someone or something — a shared enemy — to channel pain and grief. But we couldn't turn on one another. We couldn't let *why* lead to blame and finger-pointing amongst ourselves. Sowing distrust and pitting employees and managers against one another, pitting co-workers against one another, could rip our organization apart. And it could fray the legacy of public trust we'd held as an organization for more than 100 years.

We needed to stay intact and unified if we had any chance of repairing and healing. We would need to draw on our strength, reflecting every bit of goodness and compassion and empathy we felt toward one another. We could not forget that we were collectively part of something much larger than ourselves.

And we would not be able to unify ourselves by rallying in common anger against Mario, as we might have if he'd been an outside enemy, an Other. Because he wasn't an outsider, he'd been a beloved insider.

He was ours, too.

Standing In

FTER THE PRESS CONFERENCE, the joint Incident Command Center began to shift toward the work of wrapping up and preparing for the Press Q&A. The police would handle the crime scene, coordinate with the coroner, and launch a broader investigation. It was time for us to move into the next phase of crisis management, both to navigate the logistics of the current situation and to establish a pathway for repair and return to normalcy. Well, normalcy of operations anyway. Returning to normalcy, in general, seemed hard to imagine.

We'd developed policy and procedure templates for disaster recovery, and used them many times, but in 2009, we didn't have specific checklists or guidelines for an on-site shooting. This was before the almost-daily reports of shootings at schools, churches, theaters, and workplaces. Before we'd all become aware that gun violence could happen anywhere, to anyone, at any time, without warning. Before the rare, but increasingly real possibility of gun violence had instilled an undercurrent of angst into everyday life. This was new territory for us all.

As the joint Incident Command Center began to disband, we formed a smaller Crisis Ops Task Force and reverted to our default location in the main hospital. At the first meeting, we received and discussed reports from the key departments that had been most involved in managing the immediate event.

Our security team had already reached out to a firm specializing in violence assessment and prevention. They'd be onsite by early evening. We needed to quickly determine if there were further risks and evaluate the policies and procedures we currently had in place. We were already beginning to hear questions challenging the adequacy of our employee background checks, concerns that the Outpatient Pharmacy didn't have bullet-proof glass, and opinions that the security guards in the lobby should have been armed.

A process had been established for providing crisis counseling, and trained psychologists and therapists were being brought in to augment our own team's expertise. Calls from social workers and chaplains from across our health system and from neighboring hospitals had flooded the phone lines to offer additional help and support. And though ongoing counseling would be voluntary, we'd need to widely assess the psychological impact of the shooting. We'd need to specifically seek out those who were most severely affected and ensure they got the help they needed.

Members of the pastoral care team were assigned to each family, both to offer immediate spiritual support and comfort, and to assist with logistics and wayfinding as additional family members began to arrive at the hospital. It was incredible to witness the level of care and compassion that they provided, not only that evening, but for weeks and months to come. And in the face of their own grief and loss at the death of their colleagues.

Naturally, the chaplains would be instrumental in planning and conducting the onsite memorial services and in helping us all begin to heal. But beyond their role as spiritual "liaisons," they'd also serve as operational liaisons as well. Alongside representatives from human resources, they'd be integral in helping the families navigate through post-employment procedures — like arranging for the return of our employees' personal items, filling out worker's compensation forms, and processing employer-sponsored life insurance claims — which, under these circumstances, were unusually complicated and emotionally-challenging for all involved.

Obviously, these weren't typical employee separations. We'd find out just how difficult it was to anticipate all the potential complications, and how difficult it would be to walk the fine line between helping the family members file required paperwork, while not offending or intruding with overly bureaucratic details. As much as we wanted to make the necessary administrative process easy and error-free for them, we'd find that it was much more difficult than we'd hoped.

One significant area of concern was making sure the families weren't billed for any of the medical services their loved ones had received. It was an unusual situation — where they'd been shot and where they'd received emergency care, were one and the same. We could only imagine what a terrible emotional blow it would be if one of the victim's families were to later open mail that contained a bill from us. It would seem simple to prevent this from happening. But, in addition to receiving a bill from the hospital, we'd have to ensure that all the private-practice surgeons and associated pathologists, anesthesiologists, and emergency room doctors put their billing processes on hold too. Because when a patient is hospitalized, more than one bill is generated — one from the hospital and several more from each of the doctors who had provided care. And though we'd thought of this in advance and put a process in place to stop all billing, one would accidentally and inadvertently slip through six months later. One for 50 pints of blood. And I would find out just how insensitive and incompetent we appeared, and how re-traumatizing it was for all.

In the time remaining in the Crisis Ops meeting, we discussed the critically important next phase of external and internal communication. And while losing a job didn't compare to losing your life, this was the second trauma the organization had recently experienced — the other being the layoff and the stress leading up to it. We wanted to be clear and forthcoming, consistent and compassionate, and, this time, share as much information as possible.

We would need a multitude of strategies — memos, in-person rounding, town halls, and small group meetings — to reach our large workforce, which was spread across many sites and worked around the clock. We called for an All-Management Team meeting to be held within the next hour to provide an overview of the facts as we knew them, and an outline of the interventions planned for the days ahead. And to ensure broad communication to the whole health system, we arranged to film a webcast first thing the next morning.

Our regulatory affairs department had begun the process of notifying the relevant agencies to file official reports, coordinate site visits, and implement corrective action, as needed. The Department of Health & Human Services and OSHA (Occupational Safety & Health Administration) were just two of many we were required to immediately inform.

As a process-intense organization directly responsible for people's lives, we were accustomed to rigorous scrutiny and frequent inspections by external evaluators. It would be an exaggeration to say that we enjoyed them, but under normal circumstances, we did see inspections as important double-checks of our operational systems. We viewed them as opportunities to validate our processes, reveal areas needing improvement, and actively identify ways to increase precision and accuracy in order to prevent errors and adverse outcomes. We had embraced the philosophy that "we didn't know what we didn't know" and that exposure was far better than remaining blind to our weaknesses. I was proud that in past situations, we had been able to move past the initial fear of being found at fault when something bad happened, and we'd been able to focus on improvement and prevention, so that it didn't happen again. It was one of the aspects of our organizational culture that I'd most admired.

So, while it was in this spirit that we contacted nearly a dozen agencies to self-report, I was apprehensive that our team would have to undergo what I expected would be intense interrogations. I worried about the impact of re-living the trauma. Processing it would have therapeutic benefits, of course, if done with experts at the right time and in the right place. But, in the context of an investigation, we could very well find ourselves in the position of defending our actions as an organization. And I anticipated the possibility that we'd also have to account for the actions of our own employee. As a large, acute care trauma center, we'd been through situations where death had occurred and a mistake or error or negligence was suspected as a root cause, but none of us had experience with this kind of death — murder done to one of us, by one of us.

At the end of the hour, we wrapped up and adjourned so that we could head over to the theater for the All-Management meeting. We agreed that for the foreseeable future, this smaller Crisis Ops team would meet twice daily, at 8am and 4pm in my office. We'd find that establishing order and structure — organizing ourselves to tackle the details and having a common focus — was one way to cope with grief. I was amazed at our capacity as a group to absorb, overcome, manage, and keep moving. Taking definitive, constructive action allowed us to temporarily compartmentalize the severe, potentially paralyzing emotions we felt. It distracted us, initially, from the fear of what lay ahead.

***

As I descended the carpeted steps to the floor-level stage of our indoor theater, I saw that the large room was nearly filled to its capacity. Like a movie theater, the seating was stadium style, the walls were covered in sound- and light-absorbing material, and an enormous projection screen stretched across the entire front wall of the room. Nearly two hundred members of our management team sat in the dim light, talking with one another in soft, quiet voices as they waited for the meeting to begin. It was a little before five o'clock in the evening.

We had not yet announced the names of the victims; at the press conference I'd said that two people had died, and that the third was in critical condition. I would have to tell them in person — I'd have to say the words out loud — that both Hugo and Kelly had died. I thought about the many people in the room who, like me, were close to Kelly. I corrected myself, *had been* close to him. Many of us had worked with him for 20 years. He was affable, warm, funny — easy to get to know. He didn't hesitate to express emotions like tenderness, concern, and love, and, because of that, he'd bonded easily with people. While we'd known Hugo for less time, the same was true of him. He was a deeply dedicated family man, intensely engaging, vibrant, serious, and driven to be the best he could be. He gave life his all. And, of course, I've already told you about Mario. I didn't doubt that many in the room had feelings of loss for him too, albeit much more complicated ones now.

In our long history together, strong allegiances and loyalties had been developed within and between departments and units, often crossing generations, functional roles, and traditional hierarchy. Tight bonds and, in many cases, lifelong friendships had been forged by years of shared experiences. Our workplace was a complex mosaic of affiliations and identities, united by meaning and a shared purpose, and a strong sense of belonging. We were a family. And like any family in crisis, we needed one another now more than ever. I would discover, though, that how long our work family stayed together was less important than how well it stayed together.

I continued down the left-side aisleway of the theater, scanning the room and greeting many with a silent nod, or a touch to the shoulder, as I passed. Their eyes intensely searched mine for a glimpse of hope, as though looking for an indication that I might instead surprise them with good news, rather than with the news they already, deep-down, knew was coming. It was as though they were willing me to not say the words that we all dreaded to hear. Willing me, instead, to maintain the fantasy that somehow Kelly had survived. Or, to at least postpone or suspend reality, until we all had a chance to catch up to it.

I reached the bottom of the stairs, turned to face the entire crowd above me, and stood alone on the stage. There was no podium between us. I was unscripted. I told myself that I'd wait a few more minutes for everyone to completely settle into their seats. And for them to absorb the news I'd essentially shared as I'd made my way, wordlessly, down the stairs. News that I wore on my face. But mostly, I paused to gather my courage. I looked up at hundreds of my colleagues and took it all in — the collective countenance of sadness and despair that surfaced as reality reluctantly sank in. I knew that they now knew I wouldn't be sharing any good news.

Earlier in the day I had heard the stark, terrifying sounds of fear; now I was staring directly into the faces of loss. In a flash, I became profoundly aware of a unique consequence of traumatic loss on a family system. A consequence that I'd never personally experienced. In that moment, I now understood how tragic loss could pull people closer together and, simultaneously, push them apart. Especially when the loss was sudden and unexpected and violent. Especially when the assailant was another member of the group. And especially if there was blame. Regardless of whether the blame was real or perceived, overt or subliminal, other- or self-directed.

On the one hand, having a family that comforted and supported one another was sometimes the only way individual members could survive a loss — and often the whole was further strengthened in the process. But sometimes the individual survivors also served as constant reminders to one another of what had been lost, how it had been lost, and why it had been lost. Constant reminders of the unbearable pain they each bore.

In that moment, I understood completely why many of the people closest to this tragedy would not be able to stay, why they'd need to leave. And I thought being aware of this unique tension — the "push and pull" of traumatic loss — would save me. I thought I could overcome it. I thought it would be different for me.

I'd shared nearly two decade's worth of memories with most of the people in the room, but this singular image of my colleagues' traumatized faces was now seared into my mind's eye. And no matter how hard I'd try to resist, almost every time I faced them in the future, this exact moment would be instantly recalled, and feelings of loss would be involuntarily triggered. The loss of our collective innocence and the loss of those who had been violently taken from us. On my watch. And I would come to understand just how strong the forces of "push and pull" could be.

After a few minutes, I began speaking to my colleagues. My team. My friends. My work family. The part of me that needed to summarize, inform, and report the facts — to say the words, "Kelly and Hugo died" — felt separate and distant, as though I were outside my body, calmly observing myself. But the part of me that wanted to comfort, that felt compelled to rally and unify us, emerged extemporaneously from deep within, fully connected and present. I toggled between these two states, relying on both parts to wholly function.

And as I stood before them, I also saw the distinct look of fear as the realization settled in that one of our own employees had killed his bosses. Of course, there would be questions. Was anyone else involved? Were there accomplices? Were managers being targeted? Were managers in danger? I understood why the motive would have to be central to the investigation, but my worry deepened that the search for the motive could create deep divisions between staff and management. That it would cause us to question our culture in ways that could cause more harm, rather than healing. In the process of getting to the answers, we would need to manage the fear that we all, understandably, now felt.

It takes a team, of course, to manage catastrophe or tragedy. But standing there that day, I realized the critical importance of having someone visibly and overtly assume the role of point person to ensure unity when confusion and fear threatened to unravel the organization. A person to "Stand In," unflinchingly and without hesitation, when faced with uncertainty, extreme ambiguity, or unwanted change. Even when afraid, even when there was no guarantee of a positive outcome. To "Stand In" meant sometimes being the lightning rod. Sometimes being the protector. Sometimes the defender. To *"Stand In"* meant taking the heat — absorbing and containing it — without deflection or avoidance. To 'Stand In' meant shielding others from harm whenever possible. And never causing more harm.

The events of that day, and their aftermath, would test all that I had believed about leadership, redefining what it meant to lead through tragedy, and even changing the way I led in routine, every-day circumstances thereafter. *Standing In* became my private code phrase, a signal to lead with equanimity and resolve, through the din of tumult and chaos, whenever we were faced with adversity. To do, and to be, what was called for, even when blame or hiding felt easier. Especially then.

And from that day forward, I never again felt self-conscious about calling this group my family. I had discovered the importance of naming what you treasure.

***

Once the All Management meeting adjourned, I began rounding like I'd done at the start of the day. But this time I encountered people in varying degrees of sadness and disbelief, still shaken by the day's events. Some described the terror of sheltering in place — hiding behind barricaded doors for more than an hour — while they waited and wondered and worried. Though most had been far removed from the violence and hadn't heard the gunshots or the screams, everyone talked about the anxiety and fear they'd felt as reports of the shooting had initially spread through the organization.

Fortunately, though, a large majority of our staff had not been witnesses or anywhere near the crime scenes during or after the shooting. An uneasiness would linger for a time, but I could see the signs of rebound and a fierce determination to not be derailed by fear. Our staff had already begun to make the transition to normalcy by focusing on their work and caring for their patients.

As Shift Change began at 7pm, I stood at the base of the pedestrian bridge linking the employee parking structure to the main hospital to greet incoming night staff and say goodbye to those who had served through an extremely difficult day. I continued rounding in the hospital over the next three hours, visiting every unit and department, updating the newly arrived staff members and getting insight into what had been reported outside the hospital. There were lots of questions and speculation about possible motives, which was to be expected in any environment, but especially in ours, where having a diagnosis and determining an etiology were second-nature activities. And where conducting Intensive Assessments and root cause analyses were commonplace practices after an error or sentinel event. Retrospection was in our organization's DNA.

Throughout the evening I also met with the families of the victims and shooter and was met with overwhelming grief and frustration. Naturally, they, too, wanted answers and information — of which we still had little. It was hard not to take their anger personally as the leader of the organization responsible for safeguarding their loved ones' health and safety. That their loved ones had been murdered at work, at a place that they thought was safe, was nearly impossible to understand, let alone, accept. And for one family, having to accept that their loved one had done the murdering, presented its own unimaginable agony.

Though I was meeting many of the family members for the first time, I was struck by how much I knew about them — mostly through the stories and photos that Kelly and Hugo had proudly shared over the years. Offering condolences — the ubiquitous "thoughts and prayers" — seemed shallow and insufficient; I hoped they knew how much I cared, even though my words seemed inadequate to me. Like so many tragedies, there was nothing that could really be done at that moment to fix it or change what had happened. Or to make it better. I could only be with them, bearing witness to their grief, while doing my best to manage my own. But it didn't help that I didn't have any answers about why it had happened.

At around 11pm, I left the main hospital and walked alone across the bridge to the parking lot. Outside, it was eerily quiet, almost serene. The air was as still and calm as it had been when I'd arrived in the morning. The sky clear and cloudless. The night seemed oblivious to the perfect storm that had blown through during the day.

I walked past Kelly's parked car on the way toward mine. I imagined that at any moment he'd come walking up behind me to retrieve it for his drive home. I imagined us standing beside it, chatting and catching up at the end of a long day, like we'd done so many times before. But a split second later, I was abruptly gripped by reality, and the immense sadness that came with knowing why that would not be happening tonight. Why it would never happen again.

It seemed strange to leave his car behind, knowing it would stay there all night and be in the same place when I returned in the morning. Personified, it seemed forlorn and lonely, left alone in the dark, cold, quiet night. It would take a few days for arrangements to be made to have it returned to his home. For the next several years I'd find myself looking for his car almost every time I walked to and from the lot. And I would be startled every time I saw one like it.

As I drove home late that night, tears filled my eyes and streamed freely down my face, turning streetlights into glistening starbursts that distorted my view of the empty freeway. I didn't sob, bawl, or wail. I seeped. I would cry privately and silently like this every day, to and from work, for months. Siphoning a little bit of the hurt and sorrow along the way. My only true release.

Though the day had come to an end, it would not be easily or naturally relegated to the past. Rather, it would remain perpetually in view, anachronistically occupying a place in the present, where it did not belong.

Previously, I had thought of the past as a collection of life's moments, an expanding cache of events and experiences which were systematically filed and stored away in the brain and made available for future retrieval in the form of "memories." But the trauma of that day wasn't processed in the usual way; instead, it remained suspended in a swirling eddy, a never-ending *now*, even as the river of time flowed on.

Theoretically, each new day that passed thereafter should have created distance, at least temporally, from the trauma. But returning day after day to the same location, to the same scenes, would repeatedly trigger the emotions and sensations of the trauma. There would be no escaping it. We couldn't tear the hospital down, we couldn't re-locate it, we couldn't close it. The trauma would be held, undigested and unabsorbed, not just in my mind, but in every cell of my body. I'd re-experience the feelings in real time, again and again.

For me, 4/16 wouldn't be *remembered*, it would be continually *re-lived*.

"By the tragic gap I mean the gap between the hard realities and what we know is possible – not because we wish it were so, but because we've seen it with our own eyes."

~ *Parker J. Palmer, Author & Teacher*

Mind the Gap

5 Hot Wash

THOUGH I LAY MOTIONLESS IN BED, my mind tossed and turned throughout the short night. There was no reprieve from the intrusive images, no break from sharp pangs of heartache, none of the comforting amnesia that sometimes comes, temporarily, with sleep. It would be a long time before I experienced restorative or peaceful sleep again. After a couple of restless hours, I got up, showered, put on fresh clothes, and drove back to the hospital in the pre-dawn darkness.

From the second floor of the parking structure, I walked again across the bridge to the main hospital. Once regarded as just a practical mechanism for arriving and departing, the bridge had become a powerful symbol of connection and transition — of before and after — in the span of less than 24 hours. As I looked back from the other side, I also took note of our hospital's logo which was permanently stamped into the concrete at the apex of the bridge. At the center of the logo was a medical cross, and, surrounding it in each diagonal corner, were four hearts; together, the cross and hearts formed a circle. Prominent and visible to all who entered as they passed beneath the archway, I now saw more meaning in it, too. It was a beacon, a symbol of love and protection, and a declaration of the healing and care we provided.

At 4:30 in the morning, my two bosses and I, along with our internal PR team, reconvened in my office. We'd planned to film an informational webcast and broadcast it throughout the health system in time for the 7am shift change. The day before, we'd sent out a series of emails, held two press conferences and an All-Management Team meeting, and thoroughly rounded in-person. But we knew we'd need to do a lot more to keep people updated and let them know what to expect in the coming weeks.

The president of the health system and I sat at the conference table in my office, side by side, solemnly facing the camera. We began with a statement about how the tragedy was unlike anything anyone of us could have imagined. We then briefly recapped the event. We provided basic details about the three employees who had died — where they worked, their titles, and years of service. We confirmed that Mario had been the shooter and that he had taken his own life. And we acknowledged the exemplary actions of the security officers, emergency department staff, and the other first responders.

"Every employee involved in the incident made me incredibly proud to be a member of the Long Beach (Memorial) employee family," I said.

"Disaster drills cannot prepare you completely for this sort of event, but common sense and courage prevailed," I added.

"I know that everyone has been traumatized by this. Our chaplains, social workers and employee assistance program counselors were dispatched immediately to the employees most directly impacted — and will be continuously available to all of our employees who need their assistance."

As a team, we'd been well-prepared to meet the tactical and logistical demands of the crisis. After all, it was our business to care for people with traumatic injuries and devastating illnesses. But this trauma wounded us deeply and personally, and exposed emotional vulnerabilities that we'd not previously experienced as an organization. Some emotions can't be accurately imagined or simulated in advance. So, when I said the words *"disaster drills cannot prepare you completely,"* what I meant was that you couldn't completely prepare for the emotional toll of a disaster that you hadn't yet experienced. Even if you thought you could. Even if you were convinced you would know how you'd feel. Even if you were certain that you'd "seen it all." And in that "aha" moment, I was grateful that we were in it together, as a team.

"The outpouring of support that we received from all of the other campuses and the community has been overwhelming. It makes me realize what an amazing organization this is and what a remarkable privilege it is for me to serve our patients and employees alongside all of you," I said.

We then promised to keep everyone informed as more information became available and once we understood how "this terrible event had come to pass."

"And of course, we will work with the families of our dear friends and colleagues who died yesterday to plan fitting services to honor their service and celebrate their lives. More information about these events and other opportunities to support the families will be provided in the coming days," I said.

The sentiments expressed throughout the webcast were heart-felt and sincere, and, while I knew our tones and affect conveyed this, I was aware that our choice of words leaned, necessarily, toward ones that were soothing and non-inflammatory. Almost sanitizing:

The incident. As though it had been a "disturbance" or a "commotion."

This sort of event. As though it had been an unsavory "happening."

Had come to pass. As if it had been an unfortunate accident.

Who died. At least I hadn't said *passed away.*

It reminded me of when people said *"cancer"* in a hushed tone, or whispered "the big C," — ostensibly out of politeness and courtesy, but mostly out of their own discomfort with the topic. I wanted to express the anger and outrage I felt — and that I knew others felt — that our friends and colleagues had been killed. It had been the worst day in the organization's history. For some, it was the worst day of their lives. And, for all, it was more than incidental. But it was clear we were uncomfortable naming it, uncomfortable saying *Murder* or *Homicide.* Even though it was true. Or *Vicious Execution.* Even though that was even more accurate.

Because speaking about the trauma was unusually complicated by the fact that the shooter was one of our own. We didn't want to fan the flames of outrage and anger that surrounded his rumored motive. And, while we didn't want to create more confusion with errant speculation in an already tense and emotionally charged situation, we also knew we couldn't just ignore the rumors. We reiterated that the police would be leading the investigation, but that we wanted to share all that we could.

"The media is inaccurately reporting information, and rumors are circulating that the tragedy was related to the layoff that occurred on March 26th," we said.

And then added, "There has been a lot of speculation that further layoffs had been planned — which may have led to this event."

We calmly, but emphatically denied that more layoffs were intended or planned. We stated that the actions taken at the end of the previous month had positioned the health system to finish the year in a strong financial position and had made everyone's position more secure in the future.

For years I was troubled by the fact that we hadn't stressed in the webcast that what the shooter had done was wrong, irrespective of motive. That we hadn't simply and clearly said that regardless of what had motivated him, nothing justified what he had done. I was bothered that, instead, we'd felt compelled to vigorously defend the layoff and refute that more were coming. It was as if we were debating the soundness or validity of the motive, rather than condemning the act outright. As if by insisting that the layoff had been justified, we could eliminate it as a factor and negate the influence it may have had in the mind of the shooter.

To understand why, it's important that I share more background about the time leading up to the layoff.

***

In the Fall of 2008, the nation experienced a catastrophic economic crash. In the years leading up to it, most of us had participated in, and benefited from an economic system that said "more, more, more" was possible. But much of the "more" had been false gain. The housing and stock markets were artificially elevated — inflated by ego, wishful thinking, and unrestrained consumerism. And, in hindsight, by unchecked fraud and greed. Though we talked about the "bubble," we hadn't believed it would burst. Warnings were taken about as seriously as the proverbial man on the corner, who stands day after day, year after year, holding up an "End is Near" sign.

Our sense of financial security all but disintegrated when the stock market hit an historic low on September 29, 2008. There would be no "easing into," or "smoothing out," or gradual "course-correcting" toward a new economic equilibrium. Instead, the crash was sudden and harsh. Immediately, property values and equity vanished, and foreclosures escalated. 401k and retirement plans evaporated. Savings disappeared. For good reason, our faith in the stability of the economy — and trust in the financial institutions and government systems regulating it — was severely damaged.

No one knew where the bottom was, or how much further the economy could slide. Organizations and individuals alike were under intense financial pressure to react swiftly and decisively to shore up their losses before it was too late. For most, that meant jumping quickly onboard the cost-cutting bandwagon, in order to salvage their current financial portfolio and to, hopefully, preserve their future viability.

The actions taken by each would have an almost immediate domino effect on others. Most hunkered down and stopped spending, understandably and justifiably compelled to hold on to their remaining funds. But cutbacks begat cutbacks, resulting in less spending, leading to more cutbacks, and then even less spending. As though intent on fulfilling its own prophecy, the downward spiral was intense and frenzied. Few would be left untouched and many would suffer the consequences — at least, initially, on paper. Some, however, would be more directly and tangibly affected through job loss or homelessness.

A significant number of our employees' family members worked in other large and highly visible industries in our region. The Ports of Long Beach and Los Angeles, a large school district, community college, university, police and fire departments,

Boeing and other manufacturing-related companies were inarguably at risk and facing the likelihood of severe workforce cutbacks. Anxiety about "Reductions in Force" was pervasive in the community, abetted by around-the-clock talk in every media outlet and around every water cooler and kitchen table. Worry was contagious. No one felt immune or safe.

Nor was our organization immune to the stock market crash or the impending recession. As a major economic engine and one of the largest employers in the City, the livelihood of thousands of people, directly and indirectly, depended upon us. You'd think that healthcare service organizations and, in particular, acute-care hospitals were recession-proof — after all, people couldn't control when they got sick or injured. But during tough financial times, patients put off elective procedures, or delayed seeking care due to cost concerns, even if they had insurance.

At the time, we had more hospitalized patients than expected, but the number of patients undergoing outpatient surgeries and elective procedures had declined. In a quirk of healthcare reimbursement, most hospitals made money on their outpatient and procedure work, but lost money, overall, on most of the inpatient work. Additionally, the cost of materials — pharmaceuticals, medical devices, and supplies — continued to escalate. All of which had negatively impacted our bottom line. And, like almost every other business, we'd taken a big hit to our investment income. By mid-Fall of 2008 — which was just a few months into our new budget year — we were significantly behind our net income goal. And it seemed almost certain that we would not meet it by our fiscal year-end — unless the stock market magically rebounded or our revenue and expense trends dramatically improved.

As a Not-For-Profit, we didn't have traditional shareholders and didn't distribute monetary dividends. Instead, when net income exceeded expenses, the "profit" was reinvested back into the organization. Essentially, "dividends" took the form of new clinical services, upgraded facilities, state-of-the-art equipment, and additional education and training programs. And generating a positive net income every year allowed us to continue providing emergency medical care to anyone in our community, regardless of their ability to pay. Our shareholders, ultimately, were the people who lived in the communities we served.

At the time, we also had several large construction projects in the pipeline, including the upcoming completion of a brand new $200 million children's hospital tower, and the opening of a $50 million oncology center. Additionally, we were in the planning and design phase of a $1 billion seismic retrofit of the main hospital. A net income shortfall, especially if it became an ongoing trend, could put all of this at risk.

From all accounts, the economy appeared to be on the brink of a full-blown recession. Even though our hospital and health system had substantial reserves and we were still operating well within the black, it seemed likely that our net operating income would continue to decline. No one could confidently predict how long it would continue — no one had a crystal ball. Waiting and watching — doing nothing — seemed irresponsible. Incurring large losses would impair our ability to fulfill the organization's mission and put its future sustainability in jeopardy.

So, in the Fall of 2008 we launched a "Close the Gap" initiative that laid out a plan to reach our budget targets by June 30th, our fiscal year-end. There were essentially two ways to close the gap: increase revenue or reduce costs. Given the severe decreases in overall consumer spending, our ability to increase revenue in the near future was highly unlikely, which left cost-cutting as our best option in the short run. Generally, expenses could be cut in three major areas — supplies, pharmaceuticals, or labor. But, realistically, only labor costs could be cut quickly. And because it accounted for more than half of all expenses, cutting labor would have the most immediate impact on our bottom line.

With a projected gap of more than $20 million, though, the cuts would have to be severe. Initially, we calculated that nearly 500 employees would be laid off if we weren't able to make up the shortfall by other means. When it came to talk of culture, engagement, and customer service, our people were our most valuable assets. Sadly, when it came to budget and financial performance, they were our largest cost.

And in an allowable twist, we could consider the costs associated with a layoff, such as severance, benefits, and outplacement expenses, as "proforma." This optimized the optics of our operating performance, adding further incentive to using layoff as a tool to meet the budget — to, euphemistically, "Mind the Gap." In future budget crunches, I ruminated on this scheme, and thought a lot about this phrase, often substituting in its place, the homonymic "Mind the GAAP" (Generally Accepted Accounting Principles), as a wry reminder.

In January 2009, we filed an official notice under the WARN Act ("Worker Adjustment and Retraining Notification") which stipulated that when a company planned to lay off more than 50 people, it was required to announce its intentions at least 60 days in advance. Essentially, everyone in the company was put on notice, and, like most people across the country, no one was exempt from a pink slip. But we didn't specify a date for a layoff, or whether there'd be several different ones. The general assumption was that layoffs would occur sometime between mid-March and the end of June.

By the end of January, all spending that wasn't critically necessary for patient care had come to a screeching halt. We'd cut non-essential supply costs and curtailed the use of temporary labor and non-emergent overtime. We'd implemented a freeze on hiring and on purchasing capital equipment. Everyone worked long hours to brainstorm and to find creative solutions to meet the budget with minimal layoffs. Stress was palpable and permeated every encounter, every conversation, every interaction.

At the weekly budget meetings, managers presented their department's current financial performance, and were challenged to go further, dig deeper, and work harder to improve productivity and slash costs. Every face was lined with worry and exhaustion from the relentless pressure and underlying threat of job loss. But there were no signs of resignation or defeat. We hoped that the market would stabilize and that the gap wouldn't grow wider. We were determined to ratchet non-labor expenses down far enough to compensate for the loss in revenues in order to reduce the size of the impending layoff.

And, after six months — that's exactly what happened. The gap had shrunk significantly, and at the end of March 2009, we quietly laid off 43 people — far less than 1% of our workforce — and much fewer than we'd originally estimated.

At the time of the layoff, it appeared we were on the verge of a miraculous turnaround and well on our way toward meeting our budget targets, which, under normal circumstances, would be cause for celebration. But I had mixed feelings. On the one hand, I was relieved that we'd drastically reduced the number of people affected by job loss, but I was also bothered that we'd alarmed all of our employees, their families, and the community with the threat of a big layoff. In hindsight, we'd worried thousands unnecessarily.

And for a number of reasons, I didn't formally announce that a layoff had even taken place. I hadn't wanted to call more attention to it. And, I hadn't been able to say truthfully that there might not be more to come. Our financial rebound was new and fragile, and the economy was likely a long way from full recovery. But, mostly, when it came right down to it, I hadn't announced that a layoff had occurred, because I was ashamed that we'd done it at all. There had been a lot leading up to and surrounding this specific layoff that I'd struggled against. And a secret about it that I would keep, even from myself, for years.

* * *

Unfortunately, my failure to be upfront about the layoff when it had occurred created a lot of confusion, stoked uncertainty, and left people in limbo. And it had kept layoffs top-of-mind throughout the organization. So, when the layoff-as-motive rumor surfaced immediately after the shooting, I knew I needed to address it head-on in the webcast. Dispelling the rumor quickly seemed to be a precursor to keeping us united, which was paramount to improving our chances of mending and moving on.

It was also rooted in my own self-interest. Because for me, cause and correlation had already merged. The line between reason and justification had blurred. The shooter's moral responsibility had conflated with mine and connected the horrendous thing he'd done, to something I'd done.

I desperately hoped that the rumor would turn out to be short-lived — that the proximity of the recent layoff to the shooting would prove to be completely and irrefutably coincidental. Surely a note would be discovered, or new information would emerge that tied the shooting to an entirely different motive, definitively putting the layoff-as-motive rumors to rest.

But the connection wasn't solely in my imagination, nor would it turn out to be easily dismissed. Though most people responded to the layoff-as-motive rumor by saying something to the effect of "people live with the threat of getting laid off all the time and don't go around shooting people," it lurked in the background, a pervasively nagging "what if" that loomed larger than most were willing to admit.

In the days following the shooting, I heard from several senior-level colleagues at other hospitals and health systems who, while reaching out with condolences, made direct references to the layoff motive and said some version of, "we had planned to announce layoffs too, but didn't when we saw what happened to you guys." One even expressed relief that by holding off on their planned layoffs, "they'd dodged a bullet." I flinched at the remark, but the person was apparently oblivious to the figure of speech. I also received a few email messages from former employees who'd been let go in past layoffs and still had strong feelings about it and how their lives had been affected. One went as far as to write that he "hoped that Memorial had learned its lesson."

Comments like these were really few and far between — and directed at "The Hospital." I tried to deflect them and not take them personally. I knew to focus instead on the far-greater number of helpful and supportive ones. But, privately, I was unable to ignore or simply disregard them, because each further reinforced the narrative that the layoff had caused the shooting. And in my mind, each remark registered with supercharged potency, amplified by the angst I'd felt about the layoff. Moral angst I'd felt long before the shooting had even occurred.

***

Once the webcast was a wrap, we headed upstairs to the Doctors' Dining Room to join a group of about 100 people who were gathering for the official, post-event de-briefing meeting — informally called the "Hot Wash." Distinctly different from the smaller crisis ops team that's established to manage logistics going forward, a Hot Wash is usually conducted immediately following a crisis to chronologically recap the event, elicit feedback, observations, and perspectives from the larger group, and identify gaps in protocol or lapses in performance. Ultimately, the goal of a Hot Wash is to generate a comprehensive list of "Lessons Learned."

In some industries, this kind of retrospective analysis is known as a *postmortem*. For obvious reasons, we generally avoided using that slang in ours. I'd never given much thought to the origin of "Hot Wash" as a euphemism, but while writing this memoir, I came across a definition of it that caught my attention:

> *"The term Hot Wash comes from the practice used by some soldiers of dousing their weapons in extremely hot water as a means of removing grit and residue after firing. While this practice by no means eliminates the need to properly break down the weapon later for cleaning, it removes the major debris and ensures the cleaning process goes more smoothly. One infantry soldier described it as "the quick and dirty cleaning that can save a lot of time later."* (Safe Schools Newsletter from US Department of Defense)

I was unnerved to learn that the term was rooted in the cleansing of weaponry after it was used to wound and kill. After *firing*.

Viewed years later through this lens, I realized that our Hot Wash had actually begun earlier, with the webcast. I thought back on how I'd framed my message in response to the shooting. On how I'd felt compelled to defend the layoff and dismiss it as a possible motive. On how much I'd wanted to quickly remove its residue and eliminate its connection to the trauma. To remove its stain.

***

We'd thought postponing the debriefing until the day after the shooting would give us time to recover a little bit from the shock. We'd been reluctant to delay it any further, though, over concerns that it would affect our ability to recreate an accurate timeline of the previous day's event. But time, in a strange way, had been frozen, and the minute details remained exceedingly fresh and readily retrievable and, unlike those from routine and uneventful days, they'd be recalled and described with unwavering certainty and consistency, even many years later. Few of us know where we were on September 10, 2001, but we all remember exactly where we were, and what we were doing, on the morning of 9/11. Similarly, I can't remember a single thing about April 15, 2009, but there's little about 4/16 that has been forgotten.

It had also been naïve to think that waiting to conduct the debrief until the day after would provide much room for recovery, or that a new day would offer much respite. As we waited for all to assemble, Kelly's best-friend-at-work reminded me that it was Kelly's birthday. He would have been 57. A fresh wave of grief washed through me as I made my way to the front of the room to lead the discussion. As the information spread through the room, I saw that others, too, were struggling to maintain control of their emotions. It was yet another reminder that this would not be a typical or routine debrief.

We were in the unusual position of formally evaluating and professionally assessing our performance in response to our own tragedy. We were neither on the inside looking out, nor on the outside looking in; we were on the inside looking further within. It was as though we were performing exploratory surgery on ourselves, while wide awake, and without anesthesia.

On balance, we managed to remain remarkably calm and steady throughout the entire debriefing session — our training and conditioning, reliance on structure, and an ingrained habit of discipline were all factors to be sure. But thinking back, we were also still very much numb from shock — shock, it turned out, was our anesthetic.

For the most part, we adhered to protocol and stayed within the standard parameters of a debrief. When issues arose that couldn't be easily resolved, we made note, put them aside for later discussion, and moved the conversation along. When we digressed and started veering into difficult emotional territory, we returned to facts and logistics, attempting to compartmentalize our feelings so that we could stay focused on the immediate tasks before us.

But the process was messier, and not nearly as tidy and by-the-book as those sentences imply. Though we'd segregated issues that could not yet be addressed, and boxed emotions and feelings that could not yet be integrated, it wasn't hard to imagine the contents of the thought-bubbles that floated above our heads, or sense the pain encapsulated within our bodies.

The Golden(edged) Notebook

*D*OING IS OFTEN THE CHOSEN ANTIDOTE to the poison of acute stress. In the immediate aftermath of the trauma, the rigor of the twice-daily crisis ops meetings gave us the feeling of being back in control and prevented us from becoming paralyzed by introspection or overwhelmed by grief. And it kept us from seeing ourselves as victims — a label we vehemently rejected and vocally denied, and, a reality we could not accept.

There were, of course, two undisputed victims of the shooting. But there were also others, who, though physically uninjured, had been harmed. Most, like me, silently hid their wounds and pain, and, instead, claimed agency — with busyness its visible proxy.

We adamantly and emphatically repeated the phrase, "We will not be victims!" — partly as a rally cry, partly as a motto of defiance, and partly because it was expected of us. And what we expected for ourselves. Who among us has not heard the admonishment, "Don't be a victim!"? Or said it, to themselves or to others, after a setback or a loss? As though it were always a choice to be made. At its kindest, it's a mini pep talk — an encouraging reminder to be strong and resilient and to keep moving forward. But at its most judgmental, it's a warning to avoid being weak and defeated — and to keep from becoming stuck. Often laced with subtle tones of worry and fear, the phrase suggests that the slope from victim to victimhood, is, after all, very slippery indeed.

***

We existed for a time in a turbulent, dreamlike zone, in the gap between the familiar past and our new, emerging reality. We were challenged to contain, heal, and facilitate closure from the tragedy, while simultaneously operating a busy, two-hospital medical center that couldn't be relocated, or even temporarily closed. It was like the oft-cited business metaphor of fixing a plane and flying it at the same time. In our version, we were continuing to fly a plane full of passengers, while repairing a gaping hole in the fuselage. A hole that had been blown open mid-flight, when two of our crew members were killed by a third.

And even though I was leading the team and immersed in a non-stop whirlwind of activity, I frequently experienced that strange sensation of being outside myself and taking it all in from a distance. Simultaneously, I was leader and witness, performer and voyeur, participant and observer.

I had long adopted a practice of keeping a daily journal to document meetings and to track reminders and To-Dos. And though I rarely carried a purse or briefcase around the medical center, I carried a notebook with me everywhere I went. I kept a ready supply of blank ones in my desk drawer, and I'd filled dozens of them over the years. They served as de facto containers of thoughts, ideas, and observations — and it wasn't uncommon for business cards, loose papers, messages, and coffee money to be found tucked between their pages too. In many ways the notebooks resembled Bibles — black, leather-bound, with the hospital's name and logo embossed on the front cover. Even the edges were gold. I liked carrying something around that looked like a Bible, it reminded me of the sacredness our work.

As I wrote this memoir, I found myself returning to these old notebooks, less to supplement my memory, but more in search of additional clues and insights. I was repeatedly drawn back to the pages that captured the surreal period following the shooting. Reviewing them turned out to be enormously helpful, not only as I began writing about the trauma from my own viewpoint, but also as I studied the impact it had had on the organization itself. And in the process, I discovered themes and patterns that had previously gone unrecognized, seemingly traceable only in reverse.

In hindsight, I now realize that not only had compartmentalization been a protective mechanism for coping with the frequent rush of overwhelming feelings, it had also served as an effective operating strategy for navigating the complicated post-acute phase of our recovery. Compartmentalizing had helped us prioritize our responsibilities and to systematically focus on healing and growing forward. It had helped us regain a necessary sense of control.

But none of the compartments could wholly contain the dilemmas and tensions that lay within, hidden initially beneath multiple layers of complexity. Repercussions and unintended consequences eventually surfaced — some of them were the result of our actions or inactions, some were the result of positions we'd taken. In retrospect, however, most were universal to traumatized people and systems.

Viewing the trauma through that lens of compartmentalization all these years later, provided me with new perspectives and demystified many of its stubborn remnants and vestiges. By examining each "compartment" and exploring the dilemmas and tensions layered therein, I began to better understand the phenomenon of trauma and its unique impact on individuals and organizations.

I saw the ways in which some aspects of the tragedy had mirrored other scandals and crises we experienced, but also the many ways in which it significantly differed. I saw how pernicious trauma could be and how its damage could extend well beyond the event itself. I began to understand how we had been able to heal and find a path forward, while also remaining stuck in the past. But I also came to understand how, as we repaired and regenerated in its wake, we had become stronger, wiser, and better because of it too.

**

The weekend that followed the shooting was filled almost entirely with rounding throughout the campus and interacting with as many employees as possible. On late Sunday afternoon I met with the lead psychologist from our contracted Employee Assistance Program. Over the previous three days, he and his team had been conducting crisis counseling sessions with individuals and small groups of employees on all shifts. Having professionals available to immediately intervene benefited us all, but it had also become clear that there were a few dozen people who had suffered serious traumatic stress. Those who had been at or responded to one of the scenes, those who had known Kelly or Hugo — or the shooter — well, and those who fell into more than one of these categories, would likely need additional psychological support.

During this first status report, the lead psychologist presented an initial assessment of the organization's overall mental health, which led then to a lengthy conversation about the plan going forward to ensure that all those who needed help would get it — even those who didn't think they needed it. As we came to the end of our meeting — the business part was over, at least as far as I was concerned — he turned his attention from talking about the needs of the staff at-large to asking me how I, personally, was doing.

Many people — literally hundreds — had reached out to me over the past several days to ask how I was doing, and to offer support. I'd repeatedly assured them all that I was fine. My response was made as much out of habit — I'd had a lot of practice being an emotional "rock" — as it was from still being shell-shocked. And, I'd believed it was true that I was fine. Or would be soon.

As I'd done with everyone else, I told him that I was fine. He nodded silently in response, making space, in a way, for me to reconsider. This was the first private, personal conversation I'd had since the shooting. He and I were alone in the quiet room — there were no groups to address, no teams to lead, no halls to walk, no hubbub. It was the first time I'd paused long enough to listen to myself.

After a few moments, I modified my answer slightly and said that I *would* be fine. Again, he nodded along without comment, but his kind eyes seemed to invite me to say more. Again, I repeated that I'd be fine, but this time I added, *over time.* Met with his continued silence, I began babbling in a futile attempt to reassure him — and probably myself as well. I felt tears well up in my eyes as my confidence in that reassurance withered. It became clear that I was one of those who would need additional help. I didn't resist his suggestion to reach out to a therapist. I told him I knew someone that I trusted and would reach out to her as soon as possible. But, in closing, I added that I'd be fine!

By the time I got home that evening, I had an appointment for the next day. It turned out to be a life-saving step, not just to deal with what had happened, but to manage what would, unbeknownst to any of us, continue to unfold. Therapy would become a lifeline, a tether to sanity as the world around me swirled in turmoil and craziness.

When I showed up for the first appointment, I expected to be solely focused on quickly addressing and dispatching my feelings and then marching forward, as if the trauma were a discrete, containable event which, once attended to, could be left behind. As if it were truly an isolated event that was now "over." I couldn't have known that, instead, I was in the eye of the hurricane, busily surveying the damage, but unaware of the ferocious power of its backside.

I thought that perhaps after several sessions, I'd be able to discontinue the appointments because, time, I believed, healed all wounds. I learned, though, that the passage of time wasn't a panacea. Rarely is it adequate for mending the complex emotional injuries caused by trauma. Nor can it adequately contain the unresolved, shallowly buried emotions that are easily triggered to the surface in a myriad of surprising ways. The passage of time, instead, brought new developments and revealed additional complications.

At first, we met once a week for an hour, usually in the middle of the day at my lunch break. There were very few other places where I could talk freely, and soon these sessions became my only outlet for expressing the emotions that I'd bottled up and the only place to relieve some of the pressure that continued to mount. And so much more would happen in between visits making it increasingly difficult to effectively decant and process the emotions from the original event.

I also struggled to fully unpack my feelings at these sessions because I was afraid to admit to or confront some of the feelings that I'd bottled up. Sometimes I would spend an entire session talking incessantly about business or family or current events or books or travel or politics or hobbies — anything unrelated to the trauma — as if to demonstrate that I was fine, but mostly as an attempt to distract from thoughts and feelings that were too sensitive and difficult to address.

Way deep down, secretly, I felt culpable. And what if she agreed with me that I was?

But often my reluctance to fully unpack my feelings at a session was just plain pragmatism. If I let my feelings out, would I be able to re-contain them at the end of the hour? If I opened the valve to relieve the pressure, could I close it up again? If I fell apart in a session, could I put myself back together? Outside of these weekly appointments, there were very few moments in my day that I didn't have to be "on" — facilitating a meeting, representing the hospital, or making a presentation — and many times after a session, I had to immediately return to the office or go home to be a wife and parent.

On the day of the shooting, my partner had arranged for our two young children to stay with relatives for the night and through the weekend. Initially, we told ourselves that it was best for them to be away because we thought my coming and going at odd times would be disruptive to their routine. But it was mostly to shield them from the news. At six and nine, they were far too young to be unnecessarily exposed to violence, and, at the time, they didn't have unmonitored access to computers or TV, so it wouldn't be hard to keep the news from them — as long as they didn't see me. I knew I wouldn't be able to conceal my emotions from them and that they'd instantly know something was wrong. Just the thought of looking into their faces made my emotions begin to spill out. But I thought that by Sunday evening, my feelings would be completely contained, and they'd see that I was "fine."

And while some might think it's healthier for kids to not be overly sheltered from their parents' grief, I knew it wasn't just sorrow and sadness that I was shielding them from. It was also fear. I didn't want my fear to cause them to be afraid, or for them to question the safety of my workplace. Like many working parents I'd felt conflicted at times about leaving my children to go to work, but I also enjoyed my career and felt that I was effectively balancing work and home and modeling a full life for them. But how did I now explain to my young children that I was choosing to leave them every day to go to a place that no longer felt safe? It's the reality for parents who had notably high-risk jobs, but it was new territory for me. I'd previously thought the hospital was the safest place I could be.

Of course, there are ways to talk with children about life's realities, while not causing them to grow up too soon. But in the immediate aftermath of the shooting, I was coping with my own loss of innocence, while not simultaneously imposing it on them.

In the coming years, most parents would be faced with a similar dilemma as the prevalence of gun violence increased, particularly in public places which in the past had been considered safe — sacred even. But even if news of an event didn't reach our children, we'd all be forced to have difficult conversations with them about the potential for gun violence, often in response to active shooter drills at their schools. Undoubtedly, many would struggle with how best to reassure them that the drills were intended to prepare and protect them, while not inadvertently creating more insecurity and fear in the process.

My kids ended up staying away for an entire week after the shooting — it was treated as if they were on a surprise vacation that had been specially arranged just for them. They were never told that anything had happened. Until very recently it remained a carefully guarded secret that had a lot of ramifications for us all that I couldn't have imagined at the time. Though the secret was rooted in good intentions — to shield and protect them — it created distance and a gap between us that would take many years to bridge. For a long time, they didn't experience their whole mother. Part of me was locked away and shuttered, unavailable, and just out of reach.

**

On the Monday following the shooting we began preparing for the funerals. Because we were fortunate to have a large and diverse team of pastors on staff who were experienced in conducting memorial and remembrance services in addition to their usual duties as hospital chaplains, it wasn't uncommon for us to hold services on site when an employee, physician, or volunteer passed away. We'd also become accustomed to holding them for board members, community members, and long-time patients whom we'd grown close to and considered part of our organizational family. Sometimes the services were held in addition to a funeral hosted by their family, and sometimes they were held in lieu of one. It had become a hallmark of our culture, reflecting our mission of caring for the people in our community at all stages of life, from beginning to end.

There was no question that we'd be hosting memorial services for our colleagues — we knew it would be necessary to honor them and collectively grieve as an organization. And even though we had a large auditorium that could accommodate several hundred people, we knew it would be overflowing at each service. In addition to our own employee family, there'd be many people in our professional community who would want to attend to pay their respects. Kelly and Hugo had both been involved in the professional associations and had remained connected to their alma maters. Pharmacy was a large, but tight-knit world.

As we began planning, an unexpected predicament arose — would we be hosting a memorial for the shooter, too? Or not? It wasn't long before it became clear that it wasn't a simple question to answer, nor would it be an easy decision to make. And a formidable gap separated the two sides.

From the "yes" side, arguments were made that it was our tradition to hold services for our employees and that it wasn't our place to judge worthiness or withhold grace. He'd been a husband, a father, a son, a friend. He'd been our co-worker, an insider, one of us. What he'd done contradicted the positive experience and image that nearly everyone had had of him. Proponents referenced the moral high ground — turning the other cheek, rising above, and doing the honorable thing, even if he hadn't. Some people expressed outright sympathy for him, even suggesting that he had been a victim, too. And though most of the people who advocated for hosting his service didn't go to that extreme, there was a lot of talk about the healing power of forgiveness, and that harboring anger and holding onto hate was unhealthy. Many believed that not holding a service would send the wrong message.

On the other side, many were adamant that having a memorial service for the shooter would be disrespectful to those he'd killed and an affront to the families of the victims. It might create a perception that all three who had died were on the same level — an egalitarian gesture that felt highly offensive. Some said it was just too soon to forgive. Others insisted that the best way to honor and show solidarity with the victims and to demonstrate our values was by never mentioning his name again, shunning him even in death. And though most of the people who believed we shouldn't host a service for him didn't go to that extreme, there was a lot of talk about how an onsite service could inadvertently bring recognition and notoriety to him that wasn't at all deserved. Many believed that holding a service at all would send the wrong message.

Given the strong opinions on each side, it wasn't a question we could side-step or avoid. I was severely conflicted — I saw the merits and felt most of the emotions of both sides. We all wanted to honor the victims and their families, help the organization heal, and not cause further harm or create further division. We all wanted to do what was right. In the end, someone came up with a compromise that honored both perspectives and transcended a binary either/or: we would host it, but it would be held offsite, away from the hospital. Those who chose to go, could, and those who didn't, wouldn't be confronted with it in the workplace. And like covering his body outside the ED, it may have been something that graced us all, but also sent a very mixed message.

But once that decision was made, the team was instantly confronted with another dilemma — should the CEO and other senior leaders attend the offsite service? What message would be sent by their attendance? And would the CEO be expected to speak as she would be doing at both Kelly's and Hugo's services? Conversely, what message would be sent by the CEO's absence? Would that stoke further division? What was best for the organization? What if what was best for the organization, was not best, or was even harmful, for some of the impacted individuals?

I wrestled with the decision for a few days, weighing duty and my personal feelings, while getting input from others. Personally, I didn't want to attend — I couldn't imagine being there, even if it was somehow expected as part of my official capacity as CEO. My family didn't want me to attend either. They were concerned for my emotional well-being, and also for my physical safety. Undoubtedly, it would be a highly-charged situation — uncomfortable at best, with the potential to be explosive and volatile at worst.

I knew that I could not genuinely defend a decision to attend, as an individual or as the CEO, and I knew that I could take the heat if there was criticism about my absence. In the end, I decided that going would cross the line, integrity-wise, for me, personally, and that, as CEO, foregoing the service was also best for the whole. Instead, I wrote a brief statement on behalf of hospital administration expressing condolences to his family and gave it to the chaplain to read at the service. A service that ended up being attended by several hundred people.

* * *

At 11:45 in the morning, one week after the shooting, we stopped to observe a special moment of silence. Though our colleagues had yet to be memorialized and buried, we were already facing our first milestone. I'd find that marking the months for the first year, and the anniversaries, thereafter, would be complicated and emotionally difficult to navigate. At each, a persistent dilemma resurfaced: how to hold on to our colleagues' memories — always remembering and never forgetting — while also letting go of the guilt and shame associated with the horrific way that they had died. I hadn't appreciated the fine line that existed between the two. Nor had I fully understood that pushing something away wasn't the same as letting it go.

Right after the first moment-of-silence ceremony concluded, a colleague pulled me aside and privately said, "Diana, we can't let the shooting define us." She held my forearm as if to make sure I was listening, but her ardent, beseeching tone had already grabbed my attention. (That, and the fact that she was my boss). I understood the desire to keep the trauma from becoming central to our reputation and our identity — I, too, dreaded the idea of the organization being associated with the shooting. None of us wanted to become known as "that hospital where an employee murdered his bosses."

But I also heard in her words the fervent wish to not let the trauma consume us, or to make us bitter and hardened to the world. Instead, we should retain our faith in humanity, stay connected to the goodness of our mission, and in touch with all that mattered. She had a point — we were at a crossroads — and we had a choice to make in how we moved forward.

Like all organizations, our culture was made up of stories based mostly in fact, but often driven by stories that had become "truths" because they were profoundly, intensely, and widely felt. Until the shooting, though, negative stories told about the culture were the kind you'd expect in a busy, bureaucratic healthcare environment — usually gossipy, scandalous, soap opera-type dramas. Some had become lore, but most were transient entertainment. The positive ones, on the other hand, were often closely interwoven with our mission of caregiving and healing and were deeply rooted in meaning and purpose and belonging. Many had become legendary and nurtured the powerful belief that, together, we could save the world.

Out loud I agreed with her that, going forward, we could not let the shooting define us. But I silently wondered if it somehow described us. What did it say about our culture? What had our culture fostered? It hadn't just happened to us; it had emanated from within. How could one of our own have done something so awful? What had we done to cause it, provoke it, or allow it? How could we not have seen it coming? How could we trust one another in the future? How could the public trust us? How could our patients trust us? I thought immediately of the negatives.

In retrospect I realize that being able to talk openly about these negative perceptions of our culture might have dispelled myths or prevented false narratives from filling the void. It might have kept them from becoming confused with "truth" simply because they were so strongly felt. And it might have kept me from carrying guilt and shame as silent passengers. But it was too sensitive a subject — too emotionally and politically risky — to talk about. It wasn't safe to ask questions we didn't know — or were afraid to know — the answers to. We weren't capable — I wasn't capable — of leading frank discussions about the shadow sides of our culture. Not when the shadows were this dark.

In 2009, the concept of organizational trauma — that the organization as an entity itself could be traumatized — wasn't broadly discussed. Nor were there many, or any, experts from outside the organization readily available to objectively address the impact on our culture and to guide us forward. There weren't widely published "best practices" for healing the culture in the aftermath of this kind of internal trauma.

But what we could do, and this was initially driven more by survival instinct than conscious planning, was vigorously capitalize on our cultural strengths and values. Because the trauma, in many ways, also revealed the very best of our culture, the very best of our humanity. And even though it had fractured us, it also brought us closer together than we had ever been before. We'd had a glimpse of what severe division looked like and we'd reflexively hurtled ourselves in the opposite direction, back toward one another. The catastrophe had been a catalyst for overt demonstrations of selflessness and love. It deepened our compassion toward the people who were in our care. It deepened our compassion toward one another. If anything, after the trauma I saw more expressions of tenderness and empathy in our everyday interactions, as if we now held an even greater awareness of life's preciousness.

I believed that if we took charge and controlled the message, we'd overcome the effects of the trauma and prevent it from swallowing us up. If we "doubled-down" on positive attributes of our organization, we would be able to counterbalance any negative perceptions that existed or arose. We'd be able to mask those descriptions of our culture that we couldn't openly confront. We'd be able to define ourselves.

So that's what we did. We rebounded, using our mission as a clarion call. Together, we rallied — shining a light on our sacred purpose, holding a mirror up to our good work and deeds, and conveying hope and inspiration. And, in the process, we knitted ourselves together again. In many ways, our culture became stronger than it had been before.

Meaning-making was a powerful motivator and it didn't take long until I went into hyperdrive for do-gooding, attempting to reach and save as many people as possible. But over-focusing on the positive aspects of our culture resulted in unforeseen tensions, too. Most of which hovered elusively or remained just below the level of consciousness, not easily identifiable, but impactful, nonetheless. It was as if by taking on every cause and saying yes to anything generative, I could make up for what had happened to Kelly and Hugo. As if it offered a path to redemption and repentance, and, ultimately, to atonement. From then on, meaning-making and atonement were entwined, with the former seemingly promising the Sisyphean latter.

As the years passed, hints of yet another tension began to emerge for me as well. After the trauma, I had increasing difficulty separating myself — my identity — from the organization. The trauma had bonded me to the organization, and with our intense, renewed focus on calling, the boundaries between "I" and "me" and "we" and "us" had blurred and, on some levels, collapsed — a phenomenon that is apparent throughout much of this memoir. I had been swallowed up and consumed, defined, in ways I could not have anticipated. Even though I'd been determined to not *let* that happen.

***

Kelly's family funeral was held on the evening of the one-week anniversary of the shooting, and Hugo's was two days later. Both were held in churches in which they had been members for years and were attended by many friends, family members, and colleagues. Though a couple of brief heartfelt stories were shared, the Masses weren't especially personal. At first, I was surprised at how formal they were — they weren't "celebrations of life" in the way that I'd expected. Instead, the priests presented a traditional Catholic funeral liturgy with the homilies of prayer, mercy, faith, and Jesus. As a non-Catholic, I was initially confused. I'd naively thought their funerals would be highly individualized to reflect their unique lives and personalities.

A stranger at the services would not have known what had happened to them. It seemed like there was an elephant in the room. By not speaking about it, it felt as though their deaths had been normalized. How could a *standard* service be enough? Internally, I screamed. It seemed impossible that the service could hold or completely contain the amount of grief and sorrow (and anger!) that had been generated by their sudden deaths.

But being steadily guided through a ritual which was rooted in their own religious traditions and faiths created a far more personal connection to them than I had first imagined. The smooth, processional cadence of the service led us as a group through the stages of grief, reminding us along the way that those who had died, and all of us left behind, were part of something much larger than ourselves. Because, in fact, there were no strangers in the room. The words and music were calm and soothing, which not only provided welcome relief from the tumult of the past week, but also symbolically contradicted the way they had died, as if to reinforce that dwelling on this was of no use in the transcendence of their souls, or in the healing of ours.

And, all these years later, as I reflect more deeply on the homilies that had been shared at the funerals, I better understand the wisdom contained within and now accept the messages they conveyed about the healing role of mercy, prayer, faith — and Jesus. It's a strangely comforting irony that, He, too, died of unnatural causes, violently, and at too young an age. And, in a "when the student is ready, the teacher will arrive" kind of way, I can now hear more clearly their intended promise of renewal and redemption for us all.

***

Early the next week, we held services for Kelly and Hugo onsite at the hospital. Each memorial respected their religious roots but was uniquely tailored to them as individuals, giving us a chance to celebrate their lives. Lots of stories about them were shared — some of them made us laugh, some made us cry — but all reflected who they were and how they had touched our lives. I had the honor of giving a eulogy for each of them, speaking about their contributions and the impact they'd had on the hospital and in our profession. And about their friendship with many of us. Though I'd only known Hugo for a couple of years, I'd had several conversations with him about his children and family and his passion for soccer. But, as often happens at memorial services, I learned so much more about Hugo from all the other speakers — which made me wish I had spent more time with him in the past and to mourn the future that had been lost.

Kelly was someone I had known, though, for more than 20 years and our careers had been interwoven from the start. Early on we'd been paired — he, as the supervisor of the outpatient pharmacy and I, as the supervisor of the home infusion pharmacy. For most of the '90s we'd worked closely together, jointly managing many projects and co-leading through lots of challenging issues and crises. Several had been hair-raising, sticky situations, but we worked well together under pressure and we'd always found a way through. Each bonded us more closely together, and, after a decade, we had a robust collection of shared accomplishments, hijinks, and narrow misses.

On our walks to and from lunch, we'd enjoy taking turns re-telling these stories, usually adding dramatic flair and humor to our commiseration. We'd laugh, partly at the circumstance we'd found ourselves in, but mostly at ourselves. We'd often say in comic unison, "you can't make this shit up," and crack ourselves up all over again. I can still see him walking down the street, spiritedly waving his hands as he re-told a story — laughing out loud, a big smile on his face.

Both of our assignments eventually changed — in early 2000, I left mine for an opportunity at the corporate offices and then moved around our newly-forming health system, and he continued being promoted within the division of pharmacy that served both hospitals in Long Beach. But we stayed in contact, seeing each other at system-wide meetings and pharmacy association seminars. And when we saw each other, we often shared a chuckle about our earlier experiences together and always updated one another about our families.

When I returned to the Long Beach campus in 2006 as chief operating officer, we had the opportunity to work closely together again, and it was wonderful to be back in frequent contact with Kelly. In his role as the executive director of all the ambulatory pharmacies (we had several throughout the region), he reported directly to me, which might have been awkward given our past parity, but it wasn't at all. As old friends and colleagues we had an easy exchange — we could banter candidly, and we were well-aware of one another's strengths and insecurities. Both of us were willing to reveal uncomfortable truths about ourselves — and each of us was willing to hear them from the other. I saw him as a strong ally and a highly trusted advisor.

And while I shared commonly known sentiments about him in the eulogy, I kept two of my most treasured memories of him to myself. One had occurred a few years back — I kept it to myself because it was my single favorite and I wanted to savor it privately. The other, which had occurred just a few weeks prior to the shooting, was far too raw and bittersweet for me to share publicly. Together, the two memories exemplified my experience of Kelly while he was alive — an experience filled with camaraderie, humor, wisdom, and love. But they also highlighted why my relationship with him, posthumously, was so complicated.

The first had occurred while on my daily rounds. I'd stopped by Kelly's office to touch base and chat. We talked first about a couple of cool new technology projects he was implementing in the pharmacies, but then our conversation shifted to our families and kids. Like Hugo, Kelly talked lovingly about his family and had lots of pictures of them in his office. Sharing stories about our kids was an important part of our relationship. And since my children were several years younger than his, it wasn't uncommon for me to seek out his parenting advice.

On this particular day I lamented about that particularly stressful time at the end of the workday, familiar to many working parents, when I'd find myself running out the door trying to get to daycare to pick my kids up on time. I'd be frantically rushing, mad at myself for not giving myself enough time to get there, not wanting to be late, and not wanting to be the last parent to arrive. Almost always I'd make it there in just the nick of time, with a few moments to spare. I told an animated story of the rising panic and stress that came with hitting every red light, getting behind every slow car, or being stuck in stop-and-go-traffic. I comically mimed being behind the wheel, driving like a bat out of hell, and we laughed at the predicament and at ourselves, each confessing that it occurred far more often than we wanted to admit.

As I got up to leave, he stopped me, all trace of playfulness gone. In a compassionate and non-shaming tone, he said that it was more important to arrive *alive*, even if I arrived late, than to drive hurriedly or recklessly, get into a fatal car accident, and never show up at all. His sudden seriousness caught me by surprise. I laughed, thinking he was joking, but I saw that he wasn't kidding at all. We shared a silent somber moment, each of us reflecting on the wisdom in what he'd said, and the gravity of what was at stake. His words had put things in perspective.

From that encounter on, whenever I was pressed for time at the end of the day and found myself racing to school to beat the deadline, I thought about what Kelly had said, took a couple of deep breaths, and slowed down. And smiled. And silently thanked him. Eventually, I made it a point to leave earlier, so that I wouldn't have to rush. After he died, I often thought about that conversation. Though I had taken his words to heart, I realized just how much those words had meant to him — how important being there for his children had been, how important it was to him to not risk leaving them behind. His words continue to echo in my mind, reminding me of what really matters.

The other memory of Kelly that I'd kept to myself, was of the last conversation I ever had with him. It was not in-person, but via a series of emails we'd exchanged just a few weeks before he died. Kelly had reached out to update me on his team's progress toward their financial goals and was happy to report that he now felt confident that they would be able to meet their budget targets. They'd been able to substantially cut their projected expenses for the coming fiscal year by renegotiating supply contracts, improving productivity, and not filling open positions. And though they had worked hard to find solutions that minimized the direct impact on staff, he'd just announced a major overhaul of the work schedule that would reduce the need for expensive temporary help. Several people who had been working every third weekend were now required to work every other, which had understandably made them angry.

It was abundantly clear that the months-long process to "close the gap" had taken its toll on him and on his staff. But while he was concerned about the impact of these changes on morale, his emails were surprisingly more buoyant than disheartened — he was happy and relieved, he said, because, in all likelihood, they'd now be able to avoid having to lay anyone off at all. His relief felt palpable, even via email.

After several days of emails that went back and forth between us about the budget strategy, the exchange turned more personal. He wrote that it must be hard for me to start my tenure as CEO while facing a big budget crunch and impending layoffs. He said that he hoped that I knew how much he supported me — that he had my back. His exact words were "it must be lonely at the top."

I was touched by his concern and his declaration of support. I told him I appreciated his friendship and support and valued all that we'd been through together. And because I, too, was feeling buoyant and relieved to see light at the end of the tunnel, budget-wise, I brushed aside any admission of loneliness. I breezily replied that it had been a tough way to start my new role, and, though a job like this could theoretically feel lonely, it didn't. It didn't, I'd said, "because I have you."

This would be our last correspondence, and within a few days, he'd be gone. And I wouldn't have him. I've re-read this last email exchange many times over the years, pained that the layoff was what initiated it, and may have also been the reason he had died. But I was also glad to have had the chance to say that I cared about him, and to hear the same from him. His words continue to echo in my mind, reminding of what really matters.

CHAPTER
7

Check Surroundings for Safety

"IT'S BEEN TWO WEEKS!! How much longer are people going to have to talk about this??" I heard exasperation and judgment in my colleague's voice — as if those still talking about the tragedy were wallowing in it. He'd pulled me aside during my morning rounds, looking for confirmation, it seemed, that since the funeral services were over, the security assessment was nearing its conclusion, and the investigation was beginning to wind down, closure should now follow. Surely, we'd done enough to put this behind us. We could get back to normal.

My colleague was a thoughtful and constructive person, so I took the words as rational and helpful commentary, not as unreasonable or callous criticism. For most people, it was true that they no longer needed to talk about it, and, for them, the shooting would become a distant memory with the passing of time. And though it had been comforting to see signs of "normal" begin to reappear, I also noticed the unmistakable signs of tension growing between those who hadn't yet moved on, and those who could.

Caught flat-footed, I acknowledged his question with a long "hmmm," as though I'd taken it rhetorically, and let it pass by without agreement or objection. I felt a disconnect between us, though, as I was firmly in the camp that instead thought, "It's *only* been two weeks!"

I wonder now whether he'd not been expressing the opinion that we should stop mourning because it had been long enough, but, had rather been seeking some sort of permission to continue talking about it. Confirmation that it was okay and expected — natural even — to still be talking about it. And, perhaps wondering how and what to say about it.

Talking about the tragedy was key to our recovery, but it also presented a dilemma — how much should be shared and what words should be used? The first tests of communication had already occurred — we'd checked all the boxes on our disaster plan communication template — press conferences, email updates, webcast, Town Halls, rounding, etc. But this wasn't just a scandal or a crisis or reporting on a turn of events. It was far more complicated and delicate, and a fine line existed between transparency and confidentiality.

We knew we'd need to continue to address internal concerns and rumors, and to also continue responding to media inquiries, especially as final reports from the murder investigation and security assessments became available. But how could we talk about something we didn't want to talk about — but which couldn't be easily avoided?

A pivotal juncture in my own struggle with talking publicly about it had come just the day before when I attended our health system board meeting. After opening comments were made by the president of our health system, I was asked to provide a brief overview of the event and to update the board on the status of the police investigation. Initially, I found myself going into auto-report mode — starting with a high-level summary of what had happened and the actions we'd taken, but stating the facts in an emotionally-detached, business-like way.

But as I began talking about the investigation, I started describing the events in greater detail, chronologically retracing the path of the shooter and recounting both what I'd observed as a responder, and what had been shared with me by other eyewitnesses. Privy to what had been collected by the police and what had been told directly to me by dozens of others, I was holding an immense amount of information, from a wide range of perspectives, in addition to my own experience.

Suddenly, I was not just remembering the shooting, but reliving it — this time in front of more than 20 board members, my bosses, and my peers. My body tingled — I felt tightly-wound and jittery at the same time. I was present but not altogether "here."

My voice was hollow and intense as I described the gruesomeness of what the shooter had done to Hugo, and then to Kelly. And as if from way down a long tunnel, I heard myself say that Kelly had run up to the shooter, ostensibly to help and unaware of the danger he was in. He'd been shot first in the leg, then again and again, I said, as he begged for his life, on his knees, his hands up to protect himself. Executed. In the face. Hearing myself say these words out loud stopped me cold. I instantly felt danger in having gone too far, of being out-of-bounds. Of having momentarily lost control.

I immediately snapped back to the present. I looked around the room and saw looks of horror on the faces of the board members — I'd crossed the line. I'd revealed too much. There was silence. I couldn't tell if they were horrified at what had been reported, or, horrified that I had shared so much graphic detail.

In a flash, I reset myself, returned to customary business demeanor, and wrapped up my report without any additional emotion. There were no questions or further comments from the board members. Their stricken looks, though, had given way to smiles and murmurs of sympathy. They praised my leadership, told me I'd done a great job managing the organization during the tragedy, and that they were glad I was the CEO. We were back on familiar ground.

I would find this a recurring battle when asked about the shooting in other settings. How much should I share? How to keep the running visuals in my mind from becoming running verbal commentary? For the most part, I said as little as possible and I learned to keep my emotions about it to myself. And to quickly signal that I was back to normal.

Other than some cursory reports, we never talked about it again at the Board. I didn't raise it because I didn't trust myself to keep my feelings adequately contained, and I didn't know how to share the story of what had happened. I had assumed they didn't raise it because they didn't want to hear more. But I wonder now if we all instinctively steered away from the topic to protect ourselves from more discomfort and heartache. It had been too hard to talk about and extremely difficult to bear witness to the pain. It's easy to see now how the trauma had become unspeakable.

Specific references to the tragedy would periodically surface during other business meetings, too, mostly as part of planned follow-up reports. But sometimes the subject would pop up unexpectedly, catching me by surprise and triggering a cascade of feelings that I'd quickly tamp down. Once in a great while, the tragedy would be mentioned in social settings. When this happened, there'd be a momentary pause, pursed lips, and an uncomfortable nod of acknowledgement, followed by a quick change of the subject.

Some might postulate that talking about it would have made it worse by further affixing and entrenching negative emotions with each rehash. I don't know if that's true, I don't think anyone really does know, but I eventually discovered that avoiding conversations about the trauma and metaphorically locking it away in an iron-clad chest wasn't feasible in the long run, either.

***

Within a very short time — a few months at most — the shooting would be virtually forgotten within the community. I learned first-hand just how short a media cycle could be when a tragedy occurs. Perhaps it reflected our society's short attention spans, but most likely it was because other sensational, newsworthy events quickly took its place. My worries that the event would attach itself to us in the minds of outsiders and harm our reputation, turned out to be overblown.

On the one hand, I was relieved that the shooting was rarely mentioned, but, on the other, it annoyed me that it seemed so easily forgotten. Small talk annoyed me — how could people talk about a movie or the weather or the latest gossip — things that now seemed so profoundly trivial — when a tragedy had occurred? I suppose the annoyance was also rooted in envy — I wanted to be lighthearted and unburdened and, once again, enjoy "normal" everyday conversation.

But just because the trauma was no longer top-of-mind within the community, and had become unspeakable within the organization, didn't mean it had gone away. It lingered and hovered, phantom-like, amongst our everyday operations. Once the services were over, we didn't have any ongoing way to honor the victims, or collectively acknowledge our feelings, and yet we showed up to work every day in the same location where the tragedy had occurred.

Shortly after the shooting, a small group of employees and managers formed a committee to make plans for a physical monument to be built on our campus to honor our colleagues. Some people thought building a permanent structure would draw more attention to the event and that it was unhealthy to have a visible reminder at the workplace. Most people, though, were supportive of establishing a memorial, so the group proceeded. But several dilemmas unique to this kind of trauma surfaced during the planning phases, causing the group to struggle to come to a final decision for nearly three years.

Strong opinions were expressed that the memorial shouldn't be located anywhere near the shooting scenes. But others believed that well-marked, highly visible monuments should be installed in the general vicinity of both shooting sites.

Many believed that if we established a memorial, it shouldn't specifically refer to the actual event at all. But many believed it most certainly should.

Some said personalizing the plaques lacked discretion and was a violation of our colleagues' privacy. Others felt strongly, though, that listing their names showed respect and honor. Even though most agreed, a conflict about *who* to name then emerged. Some suggested that all three names should be listed, which angered and offended the rest of us.

It would take a couple of years before we could move forward with a permanent monument and, increasingly, we began to hear criticism about the long delay. Agreement was finally quietly reached. A lovely outdoor remembrance garden was created, complete with a pond and benches. It was located on the opposite side of campus, away from the crime scenes, and near the base of the pedestrian bridge. Which happened to be right outside the executive suite, and, for me, in constant view from my office.

At the very end, it was decided that the memorial wouldn't be personalized in any way at all. It became a universal place for quiet reflection, without reference to the event, the date, or the victims' names. A stranger to the organization would have no idea why it had been constructed in the first place.

I didn't object or intervene. I'd delegated this project to a small group believing they'd decide what was best. I wasn't entirely happy about the monument's location, its anonymity, and that Kelly's and Hugo's names weren't displayed in tribute. It felt incomplete. And while I had the authority to change any part of this, I didn't, because I also knew the group had done what was best for all at the time. Given the circumstances, it was as complete as it could be.

It seems unbelievable now that there could be so much debate and controversy surrounding the building of a monument for coworkers who had not just died at work, but who had been killed at work. But it reflected the complexity of the situation and the dilemmas associated with this kind of trauma. Knowing how best to remember something that had become unspeakable, was complicated.

I have no doubt that if Kelly and Hugo had been killed by a robber or an outsider, or even a strongly disliked employee, we wouldn't have faced this dilemma of whether, or not, to personalize the monument at all. Their names would have been prominently displayed as a visible reminder of their service, and as an acknowledgement that they'd died in the line of duty. As martyrs, an "eternal flame" might have also been installed to forever enshrine their memories. The organization would have established scholarships and programs in their names, held fundraisers in their honor, and not shied away from mentioning them at organizational events. We would have said their names out loud at ceremonies on the anniversaries. We would have been able to openly honor them as heroes, relieving our pain in the process, and not causing more by the silence.

And though we had difficulty knowing how best as an organization to remember them, we, of course, did not forget them.

Nor could we forget the trauma, no matter how hard we tried to bury it. No longer was something like this unimaginable or hypothetical. Knowing how best to forget something that had traumatized the organization was complicated too.

***

Throughout the homicide investigation we stayed in frequent communication with the police department detectives as they gathered information, evaluated contributing factors, and considered all possible motives. Though we'd shared a traumatic experience, we'd each experienced it, and the shooter, differently, and, as expected, there were hundreds, if not thousands, of unique points of view. Some had lots of facts and knowledge about the event; some had few facts and little knowledge. Some people knew the shooter well, some, not at all. And though few of us had access to the details of the investigation, nearly everyone had an opinion about the shooter's state of mind. Speculation about what had caused him to do what he'd done spanned a wide spectrum, ranging from pure evilness to moral crusading — with crazy, misguided, provoked, impassioned, and righteous indignation occupying points on the continuum between the two extremes.

Believing he was evil or crazy didn't provide much of a sense of safety, however. Who else among us might just snap? But believing we'd ignored his grievances or discounted signs and symptoms of his imminent rage was a thinly veiled way of blaming the victims, or others, for what he had done. And believing a decision we'd made (e.g. layoff) had caused him to kill, had its own ramifications and complications, too. How could we ever do another layoff? Of course, I wondered secretly, how we could have ever done the last one. Neither end of the spectrum of possible motives, and nothing in between, offered much comfort or security.

We were caught in a vortex in the mind of a killer — imagining and inventing his motivations, trying to figure out what had made him do something so awful — desperate to make sense of something we couldn't begin to understand. And because he hadn't, even in retrospect, fit the stereotype of a killer, we over-focused on what we assumed were his logical reasons, and, in the process, inadvertently shifted the blame to anyone but him.

I had hoped the final report would reveal a clear-cut answer to *why* that would magically alleviate my feelings of guilt and blame and would simultaneously restore my sense of safety. One that would make sense of what had happened and would give me hope that it could be prevented from happening again. And, one that hadn't been related to, or in response to, my decisions or actions.

Ultimately, I understood he was a grown man who made a choice. No one made him do it. Confusing reason and motive for cause was a dangerously slippery slope. I knew it intellectually, but I couldn't un-ring the bell, couldn't unscramble the egg, couldn't get the layoff genie back in the bottle. In retrospect, it is obvious that while I had spent a lot of time in his head, trying to figure out why he'd done what he'd done, I'd given him a lot of space in mine as well. Rent-free to him, as they say, but extremely costly to me.

Eventually, every other possible motive was ruled out. And though layoff wasn't unequivocally determined to be the motive, or even a precipitating factor, it wasn't dismissed outright either. In the end, the report was inconclusive, leaving us with mystery and the disconcerting knowledge that we would never know the truth. We would never know *why*.

***

The shooting had been what might be coined as a "black swan" phenomenon — an event that is incredibly rare, comes as a complete surprise, has major effects or consequences, and couldn't have been predicted in advance (Taleb, 2007). Invariably, however, when faced with tragedy, we are compelled to search the past for logical explanations, and, from the vantage point of hindsight, conclude that it could have been prevented — *if only* we had seen the signs or identified the pattern beforehand. It might seem the compulsion is based in arrogance or hubris, but I think it's rooted in our psychobiology. A solid sense of safety is critical to our survival — and maintaining an illusion of control is simply easier than accepting that some things are just wildly unpredictable.

Of course, I knew we couldn't guarantee safety under any and all circumstances — I had spent my entire professional life working in an environment where some degree of uncertainty was expected. No two patients were exactly alike, and no two situations were the same. There was always the real possibility of human error and a chance that things would not go as planned, but by standardizing our processes, increasing precision in our operations, and continuously monitoring and studying outcomes, we believed we could greatly reduce the odds of mistakes and adverse effects.

It was natural, then, to apply this same dogged pursuit of perfection to the safety of our environment after the shooting had occurred. Within a few hours of the shooting, experts in workplace violence arrived on site to assess the risk of additional violence, and to help us re-establish a sense of safety and security. They had also been charged with looking for gaps in our prevention and education programs, weaknesses in the existing security features of our facility, and holes in our protocols for managing threats.

The quality of our pre-hire background checks and on our processes for responding to employee grievances, complaints, and reports of threatening behavior also came under intense scrutiny. But a careful and thorough review of them revealed no additional clues or red flags. On the one hand, I was relieved we hadn't missed something; on the other hand, it was distressing to know there wasn't something more that could (or would or should) have been done. Cousin to the alluring trap of *"if only,"* the *"coulda, woulda, shoulda"* hook was equally tempting — and both were masterful at baiting us with the illusion that we had more control than we really did.

Though we already had CCTV installed throughout the facility, bomb-sniffing guard dogs, and a large, fully staffed, and well-trained security department, people had been quick to point out that we didn't have metal detectors, armed guards, or bullet-proof glass. None of these were considered community standard for a hospital, but initially there was a reactive call for all three. Magical thinking became conventional wisdom — *if only* there'd been metal detectors, armed guards, and bulletproof glass, this wouldn't have happened. And if we installed those features now, we'd at least be safer in the future. I bit the wishful thinking hook, too. But it wasn't so simple.

On our large, 54-acre campus, there were two hospitals connected to one another and dozens of outlying buildings that housed outpatient services and medical offices. All told, there were more than 80 entrances into the complex. We deliberated for several weeks about the impact a TSA-like screening process would have on the thousands of physicians and staff, and equal number of patients and visitors, who came to the campus each day. It's theoretically possible that having metal detectors at every location would have prevented this from happening within the facility. But it clearly would present a logistical and customer service nightmare.

Similarly, we considered the impact of installing bulletproof glass at key reception areas, weighing the effectiveness in preventing an attack with the downsides of such visible barriers between our caregivers and those we were caring for. We reconfigured some high-profile areas that we now saw as potential targets, but for the most part, decided we couldn't live behind barricades.

The debate about arming our security personnel, though, would persist for a while, attached to a commonly held belief that armed guards would have deterred, or been able to stop the shooter. Prior to my experience in an active shooter situation, I might have been swayed by the opinions of some gun owners and hunting aficionados. I might have fantasized that an armed guard could have at least stopped the shooter from leaving the building to kill again. I wouldn't have known how overwhelmingly confusing, disorienting, and chaotic an active shooter event is in reality — and that it's over before your brain can catch up and comprehend what's happening. I wouldn't have appreciated how different it was from the controlled environment of a shooting range. I wouldn't have known that it's not at all like the violence depicted on TV or in a video game. Being a hunter, or an ace at the shooting gallery, doesn't make someone expert at being hunted.

For several weeks after the shooting there were rumors that employees were coming to work with guns, taking their own safety into their own hands, which, of course, scared us all that much more. No one felt safer contemplating that. The police and our public safety officers did a great job intervening, making it known that, not only were weapons illegal, they'd likely cause much more harm than good. No guns were discovered or confiscated; we never knew if the rumors were true. But it raised a dilemma that is nowadays, oh so common.

I was immensely relieved that our public safety officers hadn't been armed that day — nor had anyone else for that matter. I have no doubt that many more would have died if they had. It was frighteningly easy to envision armed security guards or civilians haphazardly exchanging gunfire in a lobby full of patients, visitors, and staff after being caught by surprise by screams and loud popping sounds. And I imagined the consequences of the police arriving a few moments later to find a lobby full of people openly holding weapons.

After the shooting, I became adamantly opposed to anyone other than highly trained law enforcement officers carrying firearms in a public setting. We didn't need to get better at navigating war zones; we needed to get better at not creating more of them. But all these years later, we've still not found the answer to gun violence — the number of guns has increased, assault weapons are still available and allowed in many communities, and the death toll continues to rise. And though it's among the most hotly debated problems in our current society, we are not any closer to curbing it. We're barely willing to study it. And while there might not be easy answers or simple solutions to eliminate active shootings, I'm firmly convinced the problem won't be solved until we want it to be solved. And to date, we haven't wanted to badly enough. Instead, we just keep trying to get better at surviving them...

As awareness of gun violence in the United States dramatically increased over the years, the untested belief that conducting live-action simulations was imperative for preparedness and survival, quickly became conventional wisdom. Within a few months after the shooting, we implemented mandatory Violence-in-the-Workplace training sessions for all employees but drew the line at conducting live-action drills. Instead, for years, we limited ourselves to tabletop exercises. Staging a hospital-wide active shooter scenario had the potential to be a lot more psychologically hurtful than helpful for people in our organization. We understood the value of education and training, but we couldn't continually retraumatize ourselves in the name of preparedness. Ultimately, we were caught in a double bind — we needed to heighten our sense of security, while not creating an environment of paralyzing hypervigilance.

But the pressure to conform persisted. Within a couple of years, videos with actors dramatizing active shooter scenes made their way into disaster preparedness training sessions in hospitals and most institutions in public settings. As of this writing, there are few studies about the impact of "live-action" active shooter and lockdown drills, and none that conclusively demonstrate their value. But there are an increasing number of editorials that raise concerns that they may do more harm than good — not just for those that have been previously traumatized, but even for those who haven't.

Rooted in what felt like sound reasoning and common sense, active shooter drills and training videos were, no doubt, implemented with the intention of making us safer. But they might, instead, make us feel more afraid by unnecessarily generating anxiety, uneasiness, and heightened feelings of risk and vulnerability. Not unlike the days when we hid on the floor under our school desks during a nuclear bomb drill, gripped with imaginary fear, wondering how the wood above and the linoleum beneath could possibly protect us from the fallout.

No one disagrees that we need to know what to do and learn how best to respond, but do we need to act it out to do so? Are the benefits worth the cost?

***

Overall, the assessment of our security policies, procedures, and processes after the shooting revealed no gaping holes, no obvious gaps, no tell-tale signs. No "smoking guns." Well, at least regarding the motive. One of the things I became acutely aware of, and exceedingly sensitive to, was the prevalence of gun-related idioms in our everyday speech: *gun shy, all guns blazing, under the gun, put a gun to your head, shoot yourself in the foot, shoot from the hip, shotgun approach, stick to your guns, top gun, looking down the barrel, in the crosshairs, become a target, trigger happy*...even the word trigger was *loaded*.

And though no gaping holes in our security plan had been discovered, the experts recommended that we install more cameras in the common areas, increase the number of badge-controlled doorways, restrict access to the executive suite, and add more panic buttons in private offices. The measures were intended to increase our safety, but also ended up serving as frequently encountered reminders of the shooting and of potential danger. And while we knew that none of these additional precautions would have prevented *this* shooting, we had to consider the possibility of another, because a key finding was that we were at risk for a copycat scenario.

Though it wasn't uncommon for news of an event to inspire others, we were told that most threats were never acted upon. We were told that "those who threaten, don't act, and those who act, don't threaten" to reassure us that the likelihood of a threat being carried out was small. I didn't ask what they meant by "small," but, at the time, I didn't take much comfort from the phrase. A Pandora's box had been opened, spilling out uncertainty and the dawning awareness that much of our sense of security was a manufactured illusion. Years later, I came across my notes from the final debriefing session where the prospect of future threats had been discussed. At the bottom of the last page, I'd written the words, "woefully inept solace."

Objects in the Mirror are Closer Than They Appear

"MARIO HADN'T FINISHED THE JOB." The words were scrawled in bold ink in what was later characterized as a manifesto, even though it was, in reality, a rambling rant. Instantly queasy and cold with fear, I recoiled from the statement, alarmed by the message it seemed to convey. I scrambled to decipher its meaning and significance. Was it simply spiteful commentary, or attention-seeking? Was the writer a supporter of the shooter? A sympathizer? An accomplice? Was the writer justifying the shooter's act? Or rationalizing a future one? Was the writer a copycat? I couldn't afford, yet again, to get into the inscrutable mind of another. Instead, I reminded myself that despite what felt like an ominous pronouncement, we probably weren't in real danger. After all, those who threaten don't act. But the churning in my gut told me that my body didn't like being lied to.

Late the night before I'd received a phone call informing me that a situation which had initially begun with complaints about an employee's erratic and threatening behavior, had quickly escalated to the highest level of concern. The police were being called to intervene and investigate, and our security consultants were now recommending, as a precaution, that around-the-clock bodyguards be assigned for several of us.

Our security and human resources personnel had received a report a few days ago that an employee had been making increasingly inappropriate comments to co-workers about the shooting. The employee's co-workers had become further alarmed when drawings of handguns began appearing on the white board that the team used to communicate with one another. When confronted about the disturbing behavior, the employee had erupted in anger and hostility toward the workgroup, making them feel even more unsafe and insecure.

And while there was still an undercurrent of uneasiness across the entire medical center — less than a month had passed since the shooting — the people in this workgroup had been intimately and directly affected by it. They worked in one of our other outpatient pharmacies (we had three), which was located across the street from the Emergency Department and in the building where Kelly's office had been. He had been their boss and he'd been killed right outside. And many of them had been first responders. Understandably, they were still reeling and on edge.

Given our size, it wasn't uncommon for staff to encounter belligerent patients or visitors, though outright threats were rare, and none had ever materialized into serious bodily harm. But it was highly unusual that the source of perceived danger was a fellow staff member. Or, at least it had been prior to the shooting. Inarguably it was a troubling, but delicate and sensitive situation. No one had wanted to under- or over-react, so initially the threat assessment team had been called to interview those involved, and to advise security and human resources on next steps.

The discovery of the manifesto attributed to the employee, however, had rattled everyone and taken the response to a new level. In it were rambling, but overt references to the shooting, and angry rants about hospital administration that mentioned a former CEO and me by name, but stopped short of explicitly naming us as targets, now or then. It wasn't immediately clear whether the employee was angry about the shooting, or was angrily justifying it, but either way, the writer expressly held us accountable for the shooter's actions.

Early the next morning, a bodyguard greeted me outside my home. We shook hands and introduced ourselves, but I avoided eye contact with him, believing that his eyes might confirm the validity or seriousness of the threat. I wanted to believe that we were just following protocol and acting with an abundance of caution. He followed me to work and escorted me from the parking lot to my office, where I met with half a dozen members of the security team to discuss the next steps for the investigation and the logistics of this new security detail. They went as far as asking me, very Secret Service-like, to come up with a codename for them to use when referring to me. I listened silently to their instructions, still a bit stunned, still in a bit of a fog. I wanted them to tell me there was nothing to worry about, but concern was written all over their faces.

It was then that the security team shared another chilling fact with me: the only day that the employee who had written the manifesto had ever called in sick, was on April 16, 2009 — the day of the shooting. It was hard not to wonder whether the employee had prior knowledge of the shooting — or had been in on the planning. Had the employee had second thoughts and backed out at the last minute? I wanted to believe it was much more likely a coincidence than a conspiracy. But given what had been written in the manifesto, it was impossible to not jump to the conclusion that there'd been an accomplice and that more people had been originally targeted.

Having to interpret and respond to threatening behavior from an employee so soon after the shooting was unnerving, in and of itself, but the knowledge that the behavior seemed to be directly linked to it, had compounded my distress into outright fear. It was impossible to not view the situation — and judge it and react to it — through the lens of the trauma I'd experienced the month before. Now, more than ever, I needed the objectivity and advice of outside experts. We all needed to feel safe again.

***

Prior to this new threat, I'd just begun to settle, for the most part, into a new, post-shooting mindset of positive, action-oriented thinking in an effort to reclaim a sense of safety and security. Like many around me, I compensated by staying busy, and was determined to stay in touch with all the good and positive things we were doing in the organization.

Admittedly though to keep from being sucked into a whirlpool of fear and worry, I occasionally toggled between denial and bargaining, and sometimes I bounced between reality and twisted logic. I'd periodically tell myself that since the worst had already happened, nothing that bad could ever happen again, as though we were now indemnified from future tragedies. It reminded me of a memorable scene in the movie, "The World According to Garp." Garp and his wife have decided to move and are out-and-about with a real estate agent, touring homes for sale. Just as they're about to enter one, a small plane falls out of the sky and crashes into it, shocking them all. The house, burning and all but destroyed, is seemingly now worthless and undesirable. But Garp immediately and confidently says, "I'll take that one!" It's as though he believes the house is now the perfect place to buy because the odds of a plane crashing into it twice are inconceivably tiny.

When the indemnity fantasy bubble eventually popped with the realization that the probability of a different kind of devastating event was entirely independent of the prior one, I tried to assuage fears of another tragedy by reminding myself that the chances of *any* bad thing happening were still incredibly small. But "small" was no longer very reassuring. Small *felt* different now. I likened it to how the infinitesimally small odds of winning the lottery must feel very different after you've actually won it, compared to how you feel if you've never won it. And how the beliefs associated with those same small odds could understandably shift thereafter, from "nearly impossible" to "meant to be."

At other times, I'd lapsed into fantastical thinking that the shooting hadn't really happened at all — that it had to have been just a bad dream. A really horrible dream. Around the medical center little physical evidence of it remained — the caution tape had been removed, the flower shrines had wilted, candles burned down — all of it had been swept away. For brief moments, I could pretend that nothing had happened. But then I'd come around a corner into the main lobby of the hospital and see the Outpatient Pharmacy still locked and shuttered. Sometimes I'd get a glimpse of the construction workers inside, busily repairing and remodeling, and think about how the process mirrored the repairing and remodeling we were experiencing, including the locked and shuttered part.

Initially, we thought the Outpatient Pharmacy would stay closed for a couple of weeks, but that time soon flew by, and then another couple of weeks passed, and, still, it felt too soon to re-open. We considered closing it permanently or moving it, but eventually, in the spirit of "the show must go on" — and an equally naïve show of resilience — we decided that we would re-open it in early June.

What we hadn't considered at the time, though, was that it would become an unavoidable fixture of complicated memories and a constant reminder of a tragic event. This was before the increased frequency of shootings in public places and widespread media coverage of them had brought awareness of this dilemma to a broad audience. We hadn't learned from others that, if possible, it was best to tear down or re-purpose the site where a shooting like this had occurred.

***

On the first evening of around-the-clock security detail, the guard assigned to me did a full inspection of our home, surveyed the front and back yards, and examined all points of entry, looking for areas of weakness or vulnerability. He alerted our neighbors, informed the local police, and educated us on what to do if someone showed up at the house unexpectedly.

Each night for an entire month, the guard parked a few houses down the street with our house in full view, partly to maintain some level of discretion within the neighborhood, but mostly to keep the kids from becoming aware of this latest situation. We didn't want to alarm them, so we pretended nothing was wrong. Once the kids went to bed, he'd pull his large, imposing truck across the driveway to create a physical barricade. In the mornings, he'd follow me to work and escort me from the parking garage to my office and follow me everywhere I went on campus.

It didn't take long for it to feel like he'd become an important part of my daily life; there's a special intimacy that's created with someone whose sole purpose is to protect you and your family, and I was grateful and appreciative of his reassuring presence. But over time, his presence also kindled the feeling that danger was always lurking. It kept worry and fear constantly in the forefront of my mind and body. The sanctuary I'd felt at the hospital had been disrupted the month before, and now my home no longer felt like a sanctuary either. Instead, over time, it began to feel like a fortress. We grew the hedges high around the perimeter, installed cameras, and enclosed our front entry with solid gates.

After a thorough, month-long investigation, the experts concluded that the threats weren't specific enough to result in criminal charges. Though no additional evidence had surfaced or been discovered, there also wasn't enough information to convince us that the employee's behavior had just been harmless or ill-conceived acting out either. And while there was no doubt the threatening behavior violated our policies on conduct, it tested the strength of "zero tolerance" and our position that there were consequences to making threats, even if the person later insisted that the threats had been unintended or empty. Like other organizations, we would be challenged in the future with more of these kinds of cryptic threats, especially with the rise of social media, where conduct that terrorizes others is often defended as freedom of expression.

In the end, there was separation, and additional steps were taken to ensure that no further contact was allowed. The final decision brought relief, but I also admit I was worried at the time that taking strong action could further provoke or anger the employee. This concern would have likely arisen even under normal circumstances but was intensified in the wake of the shooting. And though fear of retaliation couldn't overly influence or inform our decisions, we had to grapple with these real fears — fears that in the past would have been labelled irrational or exaggerated, and immediately discounted. I practiced telling myself, again and again, that "those who threaten, don't act, and those who act, don't threaten."

***

Having reached as much resolution as possible on this latest threat, we discontinued the personal 24/7 security detail. But for years we continued to post uniformed guards or discreet plainclothes security at all large events and town hall meetings. Every time we'd get to the point of discontinuing the practice, a new threatening circumstance would arise, and there'd be renewed impetus to maintain what, for us, had become routine practice.

The increased security presence highlighted a dueling tension. On the one hand, it symbolized strength and safety, but on the other, it served as an ever-present reminder of why additional safeguarding was required. It was an unrelenting reminder that we could become victims.

As I examined my beliefs and feelings many years later and reflected on what I'd heard from so many others who had also experienced trauma, I came to more deeply understand my conflict with, and vigorous avoidance of, the word *victim*. I hadn't needed to permanently own the label to heal, but the staunch denial of it stood in the way of true healing for me, and I'm sure, for many others. And for the organization itself. I learned, though, that some things couldn't be rushed or forced. And, I came to realize that there had been many other reasons for my rejection of the label — reasons beyond a conditioned response or an earnest desire to channel bravado and resilience.

I had avoided the label because of the guilt I felt for surviving. I had avoided it because there was no physical evidence of my wound. And I had avoided it because it felt rude and impolite to call attention to invisible injuries when two of my colleagues had suffered fatal ones. What had happened to them was so much worse. I was lucky and grateful to be alive. How dare I encroach?

But lurking beneath these reasons for avoiding the label had been yet another, more deeply-seated one — one that I can only claim for myself because I never had any conversation about it with any of the others... though I don't doubt that a few of them felt similarly.

For me, the word *victim* triggered intense feelings of helplessness and fear and left me with an intolerable feeling of vulnerability that I would struggle with for years. I'd believed in the past that fear was something mostly in your mind. It could be managed, conquered, and overcome — it was "False Evidence Appearing Real." Prior to the shooting, I'd thought I had a pretty large and ever-expanding capacity for vulnerability. Moving alone to a strange new city, taking a job where I didn't know anyone else, public speaking, coming out, and raising children, were, I thought, some good examples of when I'd embraced vulnerability and grown from the experience. Understandably, I thought of vulnerability as a tool and mindset that facilitated growth, authenticity, and connection, and over the years, I had intentionally stretched my limits by taking emotional risk, exposing myself to uncertainty, and challenging myself to step outside my comfort zone. And, I had regularly patted myself on the back for having the courage to do so.

But in one fell swoop, the trauma exposed the stark reality of danger and violent death and blew right past my previous thresholds for vulnerability. I became keenly aware of the thin line between vigilance and vulnerability. Vigilance made me feel safer, perhaps safer than I really was. But it also made me feel more vulnerable, and perhaps more vulnerable than I really was.

The additional threat — and not knowing conclusively whether the employee was a copycat or an accomplice, or just misguided and disturbed — compounded my feelings of fear and uncertainty. Until then I hadn't fully appreciated how vital a sense of safety and security was to my everyday peace of mind. And how tenuous existence felt, once it had been shattered.

I'd thought emotional shattering happened if you weren't strong or resilient enough, and if shattered, you'd be irreparably broken and crushed, reduced to millions of pieces or slivered fragments, and incapable of functioning and performing. But, while I had lost firm connection to a sense of normalcy and "solid ground," I could still function, and in many ways, would go on to perform with more strength, conviction, and resolve than I had before...at least for a while. Well, for quite a while as it turned out.

Paradoxically, I was both shattered and intact.

I struggled to understand the contradiction until recently, when I began thinking about it via metaphor. I thought about the windshield of a car — which functions to provide both a clear view of the world and protection from weather and debris. Because it's composed of tempered and laminated safety glass, it's durable and strong, and often remains intact, even when smashed. Metaphorically, the "windshield" through which I viewed and navigated the world — and which offered protection and peace of mind — had been shattered. It was still intact, however, strengthened by my identity as the leader of an organization of people I loved. And who I knew loved me. Trauma had shattered the lens to my worldview, but love kept me intact.

As Ernest Hemingway wrote, "the world breaks everyone, and afterward, some are strong at the broken places." The metaphor of the shattered windshield helped me to eventually understand the paradox of being simultaneously connected and separated, whole and cracked, fused and split, bonded and isolated. And eventually, stronger at the broken places.

———◆———

"In three words I can sum up everything I've learned about life – it goes on."

~ *Robert Frost*

———◆———

PART 3

Holding a Wolf by the Ears

9 The Wolf You Feed

"INSIDE EACH OF US, THERE ARE TWO WOLVES," Grandfather says to the young boy at the beginning of the classic Native American parable describing the clash between good and evil.

"One of the wolves is angry and irritable, sullen and unhappy," he says.

"It's arrogant, envious, and resentful," he continues. "Over time, this wolf becomes filled with regret, self-doubt, and self-pity."

"And, eventually," he says, "the wolf is wholly consumed by hopelessness and despair."

"The other wolf, though, is joyful and serene, optimistic and happy."

"It's humble, generous, and grateful." he continues. "Over time, it becomes filled with compassion, confidence, and peacefulness."

"And, eventually," he says, "the wolf is completely surrounded with hope and love."

Grandfather tells the young boy that these two wolves fight continuously with one another, each periodically gaining the upper hand in a war that, for many of us, spans an entire lifetime. He describes the quandaries and conflicts which frequently pit these two wolves against one another.

"Each of us," he says, "has a great many stories about this battle between our two wolves within."

"Either has the potential to become strong enough to overcome the other, or, to become so weak that it eventually succumbs."

"Which wolf will win the war?" the boy asks, no longer able to withstand the suspense.

"Will it be the good wolf or the evil one?"

Grandfather answers simply, "The one you feed."

***

By late June 2009, the Outpatient Pharmacy had re-opened, and our fiscal year was coming to a close. By all accounts we were back to business as usual. I told myself that we needed to put the past behind us and to move on, and that Kelly and Hugo would not have wanted us to become jaded or cynical or succumb to fear and anger. They'd want us to overcome and bounce back, stronger and more united than ever. We could honor them by our actions even if we could not easily talk about what had happened to them.

For a long time, I believed that not being able to completely close the medical center for at least a few days after the shooting had been detrimental to our recovery. I privately grumbled about the fact that we'd had to stay open, as if stopping had been a luxury not afforded us. I see now, though, that getting to continue our everyday operations without interruption had, in many ways, been a gift; it had kept us connected to one another and enveloped in an environment that, by its very nature, was caring, healing, and regenerative. Time in trauma was irrelevant anyway: the stopping of it, or the passing of it wouldn't heal the wounds of the trauma. It would have to be processed and integrated — and staying engaged in work that had purpose and meaning, in a place of belonging, was a good start.

Our daily work kept us in touch with the natural cycle of life and death. We didn't wonder whether life would or could go on, because we were everyday eyewitnesses to its continual arrival and departure. It was a healthy reminder that nothing was permanent, and that life went on whether we were here or not. But it also made me even more acutely aware of the importance of choosing what I did, and how I did it, while I was here. And not to waste a moment on things that didn't matter.

After the shooting, routine challenges associated with the job didn't bother me as much as they might have before. In some ways, I'd been liberated from that kind of stress. I was more resilient when unexpected problems arose and less reactive to everyday business dramas that previously would have ruffled my feathers. I began to frame new conflicts with the question, "Will this be an issue six months from now?" If the answer was "no", I gave it less emotional energy. Most were "no". I didn't lose as much sleep over petty issues — and everything short of murder and threats of violence seemed petty from then on.

The experience had changed how I saw myself as a leader and altered my vision of the future. I couldn't just go back to the way things had been before, back to how I'd led before. I didn't want to. And I know that was true for many others.

In truth, we couldn't go completely back to business-as-usual, even if it appeared on the surface that we'd successfully done so.

And, though the trauma had caused long-lasting damage, it had changed us for the better, too. Witnessing the best in us, on the worst of days, had galvanized our team's commitment to our mission, and added dimension to our company's stated values — values that we affectionately called the "ABC'S." No longer did the words — *Accountability, Best practices, Compassion*, and *Synergy* — just occupy space on a page in a manual, or on a plaque on a wall; they'd been brought to life through our collective experience with tragic death.

Survivorship presented us with the opportunity to establish new models for leading and managing in the future and motivated us to change in ways we wouldn't have considered in the past. We spent much of the next year re-building our senior leadership team, transforming our administrative decision-making structures, and streamlining the flow of communication. There was a certain Pollyanna-earnestness in how I approached our redesign, as though I were well-aware that we were at a critical inflection point and eager for the chance to do things differently.

I felt, now more than ever, the responsibility to contribute my best, help others do the same, and leave the organization better in the long run. I knew it would go on, with or without me. But I also knew I could choose to make the most of it while I was here. I could choose which wolf I fed.

***

Prior to being promoted to CEO of both hospitals on campus, I'd served for two years as the COO for one of them. The process of recruiting a replacement had taken a back seat to the pressing issues we faced in the immediate aftermath of the trauma, but as I approached the six-month mark in my new role, I was beginning to feel the effects of trying to simultaneously fulfill both. And because there were also several other vacant senior leadership positions, we all felt the pressures and consequences of not having a complete executive team.

We began the team-building process by gathering the existing group to discuss our aspirations for an ideal team and to honestly reflect on what was working well and what wasn't. We talked openly about our strengths and shortcomings, and assessed the gaps in our expertise, experience, temperament, and creativity. We visually mapped our current decision-making processes to both affirm the essential steps and expose the flaws and bottlenecks. We questioned the ways in which the habit of defaulting to "how we'd always done things" might be limiting us or preventing us from performing optimally.

Throughout our discussions, four concepts consistently surfaced and became foundational to our evolution:

- Stewardship of the legacy — the value of taking the long-view as well as the short;
- Interdependence — the acknowledgement that we depended upon one another and all belonged to something bigger than ourselves;
- Culture — the commitment to maintain an environment where the best of each was contributed and valued;
- and Honor — the importance of doing the right thing, and, doing right by the people we served.

These weren't new tenets — like the "ABC'S," we'd bandied them about for years, praising their virtue in PR campaigns and sprinkling them in speeches — but their meaning was now much more tangibly-felt, more deeply-emotional. Embodied. Just as the trauma had expanded and embedded the feeling of fear, so, too, had it done to reverence.

From these tenets, we developed a set of guiding principles for our relationships and interactions as a team. The words "trust", "respect", "integrity", and "authenticity" surfaced repeatedly. But, while the meaning of these words seemed obvious at first, we discovered we didn't all interpret them in the same way once we got beyond simplistic definitions.

For example, though we all resoundingly and wholeheartedly agreed that "treating others with respect" was an absolute, its application differed from one person to the next. Some believed that "treating others with respect" meant not being too blunt or direct and never saying anything that might be critical or put someone else on the spot; others believed that respectful behavior demanded openness and directness, and that sugar-coating or kowtowing or avoidance was a sign of disrespect. Neither, of course, was wrong. It was a matter of context and intent, but having in-depth conversations about these words, upfront, reduced the chance for misinterpretation or hard feelings especially when behaviors later surfaced that seemed incongruent to our own.

And, like most organizations, we wanted "team players." Beyond being able to get along well with others, we wanted members who had confidence in their own abilities, who weren't threatened or intimidated by the accomplishments of others, and who were willing to be challenged — and able to constructively challenge others. Since our organization was a heavily matrixed environment, we wanted team members who had the savvy to know when to lead, and when to follow. We used words like diverse, balanced, well-rounded, agile, and collaborative to describe our team's ideals, but simply put, we envisioned a team that was greater than the sum of its parts.

One by one we filled the open positions with outstanding individuals. Once our team was complete, the operating philosophies and guiding principles that had been foundational to the formation of our new team were memorialized in a team vision statement that served as our North Star for years to come. We embedded it into our meeting agendas as a reminder of our belief that what we did, and who we were, made a difference in the lives of others.

But as thorough and methodical as we were in identifying the characteristics of our ideal team, there was, however, one aspect that that we never openly discussed, even though it was top-of-mind for me. I purposefully wanted to recruit team members who had not been severely traumatized in the shooting and who were unlikely to chronically suffer from the stress of the event. I wanted a team not weighed down with emotional baggage because I could feel the weight of the baggage that I, myself, was carrying.

**

Like any large, multi-layered organization, decision-making was a multi-step process, with approvals required from many levels of authority. Most operational decisions were made in the units or departments, and patient care policies were generally made in committees staffed by physicians and clinicians. But decisions affecting more than one department, and/or involving a lot of money, were generally made by the senior executive team at its weekly meeting. Many times, the senior team was the ultimate decision-making body, but sometimes it served as the conduit or gatekeeper to the local and health system governing boards for final approval.

Our overall complexity made for lots of starts and stops, rework, clean-up, and confusion. It was often difficult to efficiently manage the flow of decisions from one committee to next, get sufficient buy-in along the way, and communicate the eventual results. There were times that the senior team would make a decision, but then encounter difficulty with its implementation because few had been adequately informed. Or, occasionally, vital new information emerged in the 11th hour which completely derailed an earlier decision.

Agendas for senior leadership team meetings were usually comprised of a long and varied list of topics, ranging from small to large in importance and urgency. Some topics were brought forward simply for discussion or as status updates, but some involved sensitive personnel matters, required intense strategic brainstorming, or were requests for approval of large, multi-million-dollar projects. We weren't particularly disciplined in managing the agenda — relatively unimportant topics could easily take up large swaths of time, making for rushed conversation on critical ones. Nor were we always clear about how a decision would be made, or, once made, whether it was indeed final.

It wasn't uncommon to hear complaints that we were slow, steeped in bureaucracy, and were letting opportunities slip by because of analysis-paralysis. Other times, though, we'd be criticized for making decisions too quickly and without the input and involvement of physicians and staff.

The city we served was home to one of the largest seaports in the country, and because I liked to draw analogies, I often thought of our organization as a giant ocean-liner, and we, the senior leaders at the helm, were responsible for ensuring safe passage and smooth sailing. Before embarking on a voyage, we would need to identify the destination, determine the best route, secure adequate fuel and the right resources, communicate the itinerary, and coordinate with the crew. And once we set sail, we'd have to be prepared to navigate through changing conditions, bad weather, and possibly unchartered territory.

We could be speedy if I, as captain, made all the decisions myself with the information and advice that was immediately available to me. But even if I got 50% of the decisions right — which was probably generous — it meant that half would ultimately prove to be poor or flawed. And I'd likely have to spend an enormous amount of time and energy communicating and coordinating the passage plan with all those who hadn't been involved in the first place. In the process, I'd probably discover some crucial information that had been missing at the start, which would inevitably lead to a great deal of course-correcting. We'd move quickly, but our ocean liner would probably zig-zag all over the place, or run out of resources, or hit an underwater hazard and sink.

Alternatively, we could involve everyone onboard, and not make a final decision to move forward without full participation and unequivocal agreement from all. But even if the process produced a high-quality decision — with few barriers to launch and no course corrections along the way — it would likely be tedious and time-consuming. We'd benefit from the ideas and support of every crew member, but our ocean liner would probably be sluggish and inefficient or, like the Queen Mary, remain moored in cement in the Long Beach Harbor.

Both these analogies, of course, were extreme. We didn't have to choose between a structure that favored speed over involvement, or vice versa. We could create one that leveraged both. We knew better decisions would be made if more people were involved because experience had taught us that most of the problems or issues that the senior team faced were ones not any one person could easily solve on their own. We acknowledged that a process that was clear and streamlined would result in less ambiguity, more satisfaction, and more timely decisions. We could have efficiency AND quality. We could have mission AND margin.

**

Once most of our recruiting was complete, we gathered the new team and, using a similar process as we had for teambuilding, began redesigning our team's decision-making model. Though I've previously called out the weaknesses in our structure, we also had many strengths to build upon, too. We had experience, access to reliable data, and analytical expertise, and we benefited from both a deep well of institutional knowledge and a steady infusion of novel ideas from newcomers.

Following discussions about our strengths and weaknesses, we spent considerable time clarifying our goals. We wanted a decision-making process that was dynamic and stable, agile and efficient, and flexible and standardized. We wanted to be as transparent as possible and yet, maintain confidentiality, when needed. We wanted a model that fostered and encouraged frank, open, and healthy debate, where we could argue a position without demonizing the opposition. We wanted to know when we had obtained enough information to make the best decision and when we had reached agreement to move forward.

After talking about what we wanted in a model, we assessed the kinds of topics, issues, and projects that typically came to us for problem-solving or approval and found about 85% of them fell pretty neatly into one of four major categories:

- Capital & Construction — this included hundreds of large purchases or projects, e.g. clinical equipment, computer systems, fixtures, facility enhancements or new construction, generally exceeding $25,000;

- Operations — policies or procedures that affected all departments and divisions, e.g. benefit changes, hiring practices, managing temporary labor, internal messaging, regulatory or accreditation preparation, collective bargaining, and position eliminations;
- Contracts — we contracted with hundreds of business entities, e.g. clinical specialists, physician groups for hospital-based clinical services such as radiology, emergency, anesthesiology, and pathology, and a wide variety of support services, like food and nutrition, housekeeping, and landscaping;
- Strategy — we continually looked for ways to expand, adopt innovative technologies and programs, acquire services complementary to our own, and establish mutually-beneficial relationships with other organizations. At any one time, we had dozens of projects in the pipeline.

Rather than filling the senior team meeting agenda with a variety of topics as we had in the past, we flipped the model and established four separate committees, each solely focused on one of these categories. We added subject matter experts to the committee rosters (e.g. facilities leaders to the Capital & Construction Committee, financial analysts to the Contracts Committee, etc.) and added depth by including leaders of the major clinical service lines (e.g. oncology, cardiology, neurology) and of the large ancillary departments (e.g. laboratory, pharmacy, respiratory care).

Each committee met monthly and replaced our original weekly senior leadership team meeting. We synchronized the schedule of these four new meetings with those of the Board and its subcommittees to improve timeliness and efficiency of the process for those decisions that subsequently required formal approval by governance.

And, to keep these large, 20-member committees manageable and functional, agendas and supporting materials were sent out in advance using a standard format that declared the purpose, the time allotted, and the desired outcome for each topic.

In addition to implementing a standardized agenda, we developed a uniform presentation template to ensure consistency and so that each presenter didn't need to start from scratch. Many of the items that came forward for approval needed signoff from technical and support experts (e.g. information services, engineering, finance), so we created pre-approval checklists to guide the process. Similarly, since the likelihood of approval and the ultimate success of the project was increased when stakeholders were consulted in advance, we included prompts for this as well. Having a universal framework went a long way toward increasing speed, decreasing frustration, and, ultimately, our ability to make sound decisions.

We adopted a motto of "seeking first to understand" while also inviting an appointed devil's advocate to poke holes in the solutions. Identifying potential downsides and anticipating the negative consequences of a decision ensured we made fully informed decisions and helped us prepare a Plan B in advance, in the event an approved project didn't produce the desired results. We didn't need a perfect solution to move forward, but, we did need a complete one.

By default, we used consensus to reach decisions unless we declared otherwise. No one's vote was more heavily weighted, including mine as CEO. We defined "consensus" as each member being willing to support the majority's decision to proceed, even if concerns or reservations had been expressed. It also meant that every committee member owned the decision. If we were unable to reach consensus, the topic was tabled until either a new solution was presented and agreed upon, or a compromise to the original was found.

There were occasions when a decision had already been made elsewhere, or, would eventually be decided by a single authority and not by the group, but in those instances, the topic would almost always be brought forward as information or as a heads-up to the other committee members.

Over time, this new model instilled a stronger sense of ownership in decision-making, which reduced the second-guessing in the hallways, the chatter of equivocation in the cafeteria, and the bad-mouthing that had occurred in the past when the perception (and reality) that decisions were made in a vacuum, or by a select few, predominated.

***

And while improving the process of making decisions was significant, effectively communicating them once they were made, was equally important. To address gaps in timeliness and consistency, we altered the flow of communication so that final decisions made at Board meetings were shared later the same day at an All Management Meeting, and then with the staff at-large at Town Halls conducted in the same week. For efficiency, and in the spirit of transparency, we used the same presentation slides for all meetings, and at the conclusion of the last Town Hall, those same slides, along with a brief narrative, were posted on the intranet for all to access.

The Town Halls became a routine part of our communication process, not just for discussing decisions, but also for openly sharing the monthly financial results and quality outcomes with all employees. So that employees from all shifts could participate, we usually offered three or four options for attendance. When there wasn't anything controversial going on, attendance would average 35-50 at each. Even though that was a small fraction of our total workforce, it was a terrific opportunity for me to engage in conversation, hear issues and concerns, and answer questions directly. When there was controversy in the organization, attendance would swell to several hundred.

In a short period of time, the Town Halls became an important part of our culture. I enjoyed talking with my colleagues about the work we all did together and holding up a mirror to reflect their collective accomplishments. It was an opportunity to "stand in," whether times were good or challenging. I rarely cancelled them, partly because I wanted to maintain a consistent and reliable channel of communication, but also because I'd learned the value of getting a message out and addressing questions openly and in person, rather than remaining silent and letting false narratives fill the void.

And though we'd shifted toward a more open and transparent style of communication, the shooting remained a taboo, off-limits subject. Even though, ironically, it had been the impetus for the shift in the first place.

***

The first year following the shooting was marked by a flurry of activity. We hadn't been perfect in our response to the tragedy, and recognition of it helped us accept that life was messy, which, in some ways, served to unshackle us from the binds of perfectionism. We had used our complexity to our advantage and had taken the best of what we'd learned in the trauma to evolve how we managed our everyday operations. The time and effort spent rebuilding our senior leadership team and transforming our decision-making processes began to pay off; employee engagement increased, patient satisfaction rose, and our financial and quality results improved. But the year can't be summed up by those metrics alone.

Remember my previous reference to "Pollyanna-earnestness?" I'd thought I could outrun the trauma — and that the faster I sprinted, the sooner I'd leave it behind. I thought turning my entire attention toward the future would keep me from being stuck in the past. But in this same year of organizational reform and resurgence, I continued to struggle against the negative effects of the shooting, while also facing the emergence of new issues and complications related to it. Proving the point that traumatic growth and perpetual casualty weren't mutually exclusive.

Life did go on — but the past marched right along with it. The trauma resurfaced again and again, making its presence known in surprising and unpredictable ways. It wasn't just that I could not let go of it; it would not let go of me.

---◆---

"Holding a wolf by the ears" *(Auribus teneo lupum)* was a popular ancient Roman proverb that described an untenable, unsustainable situation where doing something and doing nothing are equally risky; where holding on and letting go are equally dangerous.

---◆---

IT DIDN'T TAKE LONG TO REALIZE that the silent movie projected on the screen was CCTV footage of the shooting. I stood watching from the back of the dimly lit auditorium, frozen in stunned surprise as the film soundlessly tracked the shooter in grainy black and white. It begins with him coming out the back door of the Outpatient Pharmacy and ends two minutes later with him lying on the street outside the emergency room. In between, the cameras in the ceiling captured a birdseye view of him travelling through the hallways of the hospital, yelling and waving a gun, parting the sea of co-workers and visitors as he approached, and leaving them pressed up against the walls as he passed. No one he encountered would have known what he'd already done, but confusion and fear is evident on their open-mouthed faces, and, as I watched, the screaming in my mind's ear joined theirs to fill the empty soundtrack.

From the hallway, we see the shooter enter the foyer of the outpatient surgery pavilion, and run past a security guard stationed nearby, before exiting to the outside through the automatic sliding glass doors. The guard, startled by the commotion and presumably alarmed by the sight of the gun, turns to follow him outside, calling out as the shooter disappears from the camera's fixed view. We see the security guard from behind, standing in the middle of the street, motioning with his hands, pleading with the shooter to stop. We don't need to guess what happens next off-frame. We see the guard recoil, and his hands go to his head in a gesture of agony and shock, as he witnesses the second murder and suicide.

Though I was well-aware that security footage existed, it had never occurred to me to ask to see it. Several months had passed since the conclusion of the investigation, and I'd forgotten all about it. Seeing the video caught me completely by surprise, and instantly triggered flashbacks and an avalanche of emotions. I was angry to be seeing it for the first time without warning or choice. Throughout the film, the 50 or so other people in the auditorium sat silently facing the screen, without murmur or movement, as it played on a loop, over and over. But that last part — the video playing over and over — is a flaw of my memory. Though it did become stuck on replay in my own mind, I do know it was only shown once that day.

I'd been invited to address the public safety officers at the Security Department's annual All Hands Meeting. Though there would be general updates, announcements, and some additional training, the primary purpose of the event was to celebrate the department's accomplishments and to recognize outstanding service and performance. I'd arrived a few minutes ahead of my scheduled time and because I didn't want to disrupt their proceedings, I stood discreetly on one side of the room, awaiting my introduction.

The entire team, including the K-9 unit, was in attendance, as were representatives from local law enforcement. Most were dressed in formal uniform. I had expected to join a festive ceremony, but as I entered the room, I noticed it was unusually quiet; everyone was already seated and staring in anticipation at the blank screen. The breakfast portion of the meeting had concluded — and the video, apparently, was intended to serve as the segue to the official agenda.

At the conclusion of the video, the Director of the department broke the silence with a few words of gratitude and commendation for the team's outstanding performance on the day of the shooting. I don't remember exactly what he said, but I do remember the emotion on the officers' faces as he talked. I didn't know for certain what they were feeling, but it wasn't hard to guess, though I realize now, that some of what I guessed might have been my own projection. I was still reeling from the video. As their boss spoke, I assumed they were re-living the stress and fear of that day, and imagined they also felt a complex mixture of pride and sadness too. Pride in their unwavering dedication and loyalty to the hospital and to one another. And sadness for who had been lost in the shooting — and that they had not been able to stop it from happening.

From the sidelines, I took some deep breaths, hoping to contain my emotions and maintain my composure. After the Director finished speaking, I walked to the front of the room and stood behind the podium. Though I'd jotted down some notes in advance, I hadn't planned to use the podium because I hadn't wanted anything to come between me and the group. But I stayed behind it, gripping it as I spoke.

Since the shooting, I had gotten closer to many in the audience — and knew every single guard by name and face. Looking out at them, it was clear the ongoing attachment to that awful day wasn't mine alone. We each had a connection to the tragedy — and a newfound connection to one another because of it. I was upset that I'd been caught off-guard by the

CCTV footage, yet I was thankful to be connected to a group who obviously cared so much.

As I finished my remarks and came out from behind the podium, the Director and several others surprised me by coming forward to present me with a military-style dog tag that hung from a ball chain necklace. Engraved into the metal was a beautifully detailed image of the hospital's security officer badge. And the date, 4-16-09. It had been specially commissioned, and each member of the department received one as an acknowledgment of their bravery as first responders and to commemorate their unity as a team. As it was placed ceremoniously around my neck, they said that I, too, was one of them.

**

Despite how closely we'd bonded as fellow employees — and as much as I'd wanted to be one of them — I was aware, and occasionally painfully reminded, that a distinct boundary existed between us. Not long after the security celebration was held, I received notice that a special meeting had been planned for a small group of employees who were continuing to struggle in the aftermath of the trauma. All had been witnesses or first responders on 4/16 — and had also been closely connected to the victims and/or the shooter.

Though each had been receiving individual counseling through the Employee Assistance Program, the therapist treating them felt it would be beneficial for them to come together in a supportive environment to augment the work they were doing on their own. There would be value in being around others who personally understood the uniqueness of their struggle and, importantly, value in knowing they weren't alone.

No one openly called what they suffered from "PTSD" however. Maybe it was denial. Maybe it was because of the stigma associated with the term... hospital workers were stereotypically "stiff upper lip" kinds of people, and stoicism in the face of adversity or pain was a prized attribute, a sign of strength and resilience. Or maybe it was because PTSD at the time was more commonly associated with military combat or sexual assault — and before the dramatic increase of mass shootings in civilian settings made the term a necessary part of our nationwide vernacular. Likely it was all the above.

The first group meeting was to be held late in the afternoon in the conference room near my office within the executive suite. The location had been chosen because it was private, but also because it signaled to the group it had support from the top. The organizer had reached out to me earlier on the day of the meeting to ask if I'd be willing to personally greet the attendees to convey that "the CEO still cared and hadn't forgotten about them." I'd said yes, and then, a bit miffed, added that, of course, I still cared and hadn't forgotten about them. She upped the ante, though, and said it would be even better, and send an even stronger message, if I were to also attend the meeting. Did she mean as a participant, as someone also affected? Or as a representative of the organization? I wondered, but I didn't ask out loud.

Shortly before the beginning of the meeting, about a dozen people began to congregate outside the entrance to the conference room. I took my place near the doorway and greeted each one as they entered the room. There were a few people I'd only recently become acquainted with, but most of them I'd known for years. As they settled into their seats, I spoke briefly with the therapist who would be conducting the session and thanked him for bringing everyone together. I didn't know him well at all but had heard about the good work he'd been doing, and how highly regarded he was with our employees.

I was still standing in the doorway and was just about to turn and leave, when someone asked if I would be staying for the meeting. I said no, and added that I didn't want to intrude but wanted the group to know they had my support. Several who overheard the question and my response chimed in to reply that I was welcome to stay and that they very much wanted me to stay. The genuine warmth and sincerity of their invitation was alluring, and for a fleeting moment I thought it might be possible for me to join them as a participant. I, too, wanted to not feel alone.

I hesitated for a moment at the doorway; instinct told me I needed to hold a boundary. I couldn't participate as an individual and leave my role as the CEO at the door. I thanked them and again declined the offer. But I'd misinterpreted the invitation — it wasn't an offer; it was an expectation. It was important for them that I, as the CEO, stay to hear what they had to say. It would demonstrate the organization truly supported them. The request from one, morphed into echoed insistence by several. No one said the words "duty" or "obligation" or "responsibility", verbatim. It was my translation, given the tone and body language accompanying the persistent request. A request that resonated with my own internal, prodding voice that said I hadn't done enough.

Every fiber of my being screamed in warning, "Do not go into that room! Do not sit down! Do not stay!"

But the dominant feelings of duty and responsibility tipped the balance against my better judgment. I stepped fully inside, closed the door behind me, and made my way, scooting and side-stepping through the narrow space between the people already seated and the wall behind them, to the first open seat, located in the opposite corner of the room and far from the only way out.

The room had always been one of my favorites — it was small and cozy, not more than 18'x18', with a relatively-low eight-foot ceiling. Its distinguishing feature was the architectural model of the medical center encased in plexiglass, which was positioned in the center of a square wooden table in the middle of the room. Because the model and the table surrounding it took up most of the room, seating was limited to the perimeter, and no more than four or five people could comfortably sit on each side.

Every seat, though, faced the model and had a birdseye view of the entire 54-acre, two-hospital campus and the neighborhoods around it. Even though the model was large — about 6'x6', it was only a foot tall, so you could easily look over it to see the people seated on the other side of the table. Still, it was the focal point of the room. During meetings, my eyes were often drawn to frequently visited landmarks, and I'd mentally place a little me, in situ, next to the plastic models of cars and trees. A habit which became problematic after the shooting.

When the room was fully occupied and the topics were heated or controversial, it sometimes felt more cramped and confining, than cozy. If you weren't seated near the door, it was hard to exit until everyone else had single-filed out ahead. And though the model sat on top of the table, its solid, immovable base rested on the floor. I was never more aware of that, than during the support group meeting; otherwise, I might have dropped beneath the table and crawled its length, diagonally, to escape.

The therapist opened the meeting with a quick overview of the common ground rules for support groups: listening respectfully, waiting your turn to speak, not judging, criticizing, or giving advice, and, of course, confidentiality. After everyone briefly introduced themselves with their usual demographic info — name, how long they'd been in the organization, and their role in it, we were asked to go back around the room and "share."

There were a few tears and some gasps, as one-by-one, each person described what they'd witnessed in graphic detail and put into words the horror that had been indelibly etched into their minds and bodies. As I listened to each narrator, I mentally placed myself into the diorama in front of me and vicariously experienced the trauma from their unique vantage point, while simultaneously re-living my own. I didn't have to guess their feelings; each shared the fear, shock, and confusion they'd felt at the time of the shooting, and the anger and grief that had lingered since. I braced against inuendo about motive, inferences the "hospital" had known more than had been revealed, and insinuation that the "hospital" hadn't done enough.

My heart pounded, my body was clenched and tense, and I held my breath in anticipation as each story unfolded. Like everyone else, I knew how all the stories ended. But we'd each traveled a different path toward that end, which had shaped our beliefs about how and why we'd arrived there.

I was hovering at my emotional edge, struggling to absorb the slew of new visual images and keep the ones I'd already been holding, locked away. I felt overwhelmed and wanted out. I couldn't crawl under the table, and climbing clumsily over people didn't seem like a good option either. I imagined curling into a tight ball, holding my hands over my ears, and screaming "lalalalalala" to keep the words out.

Being suddenly re-immersed in the shooting caught me by surprise, which seems hard to believe in hindsight. What else could I have expected to hear at a support group for the witnesses and first responders of the murders and suicide? Had I not given thought to what would be shared because I hadn't envisioned being there in the first place? Or, had I not planned to be there because I did know what would likely be shared? I think now, all these years later, that I hadn't been caught by surprise at all by what had been shared, but surprised that I'd let myself get caught in that situation in the first place.

Though I had talked in person to lots of employees who had been directly affected by the trauma, most of the conversations had taken place in the hallway, or as a sidebar in a meeting, and few contained this kind of dramatic intensity. During the investigation I'd heard all the eyewitness reports of the shooting, but most had been relayed second-hand and retold with minimal emotion. In most instances, they'd been shared as summaries that highlighted new information, corroborated key facts, and confirmed the chronology of the event, as if the primary purpose for sharing them was to fit the pieces of the puzzle together and systematically reconstruct the big picture.

I had been aware, though, of others' continued suffering in the months after the shooting — and had wanted to do more. I had wanted to be able to hear their stories and personally be there for them, but I felt conflicted. I had learned the hard way that a conversation or a report could suddenly veer into the territory of motive and trigger my own emotions, so I'd become adept at avoiding them when possible. And when I couldn't steer clear of a conversation, I had listened with apprehension, ready to deflect or divert, or, as a last resort, retreat.

I had told myself they were getting help from experts and that I needed to maintain an appropriate professional boundary. Which was true, but incomplete. Because deep down, it felt like an excuse I was hiding behind. Before I'd entered that room to join the support group, I had thought my avoidance of them was a personal weakness, even if it were professionally acceptable and advisable. But now I know it was self-preservation.

An hour passed, five people had shared their stories, and we were only halfway around the room. It was now my turn to share. No one in the organization knew what I had personally experienced. Until then, I hadn't been asked. And I certainly hadn't volunteered it. Being vulnerable was an important leadership quality, but I had learned it had a limit, especially in regard to the shooting.

I knew that recounting my own experience, step-for-step, and sharing my deepest feelings might be acceptable as an individual, but it was not appropriate as the CEO. What I could share, though, was what we had in common. I could share that I, too, had experienced horror and shock that day, without describing the exact details. I could reveal that I also continued to struggle with grief and sadness. I could disclose that I was getting help from a therapist and that I was glad they were too. I could speak about the courage and camaraderie, the acts of kindness, and the demonstrations of love I'd witnessed that day and since. I could talk about how the experience had given new meaning to the work we all did together. I could say that I understood their suffering. Which was all true, but incomplete. Because I could not admit to my raw and tender feelings of guilt and blame. I could not openly address the motive, which for me, was the elephant in that claustrophobic little room.

After I finished, the sharing continued for another hour until everyone had spoken. For me, an undeniable reality had been exposed in the process: I was strongly connected and bonded to my co-workers in many ways, but by virtue of my role, I was also separated — even from those who knew better than most, how important it was to be heard, how important it was to be understood, how important it was to have someone else bear witness. And, how important it was to not be alone.

I hadn't fully understood the phrase, "lonely at the top," prior to the shooting. I'd assumed if a CEO was lonely, it was because she — okay, let's be real, the CEO was almost always a "he" — was distant and aloof and unwilling to authentically connect. But that had been naïve, particularly in the aftermath of a trauma like this, which had been carried out by a well-regarded insider for reasons many, including me, believed were linked to a decision "The Hospital" had made.

Over the years I've thought a lot about what transpired in that 2 ½ hour meeting. I entered the room because I'd felt duty-bound as the CEO and guilty for not having been as emotionally available to my co-workers as I'd wanted to be. Once I was in the room, I couldn't help but hear the blame and accusation woven in others' pain, even though none of it was specifically directed toward me. When it came to the trauma, there was a distinct boundary between me and my co-workers, but there wasn't one between me and "The Hospital."

But I think I'd become so attuned to listening for evidence that reinforced my own feelings of culpability, that I'd been tone deaf to theirs. As I think back on it now, each of their stories contained faint traces of self-blame. A few wondered rhetorically whether they'd missed a foreboding sign in the shooter's behavior, or if they had inadvertently played a part in how the event unfolded as his path crossed theirs that day. But most references to self-blame were subtle and glancing, as though the concept were too delicate to do more than hint at, and too shameful to pause on.

I had thought the combination of being witnesses or first responders — *and* closely connected to the victims or shooter —

was the common thread between us and the source of our continued suffering. But, had the unresolved guilt we'd each felt, been the binding tie instead? And though I wonder now if that is what had brought us all together then, I do know my own unresolved guilt kept me far apart from them thereafter.

***

The space between me and the shooter, however, seemed to shrink. At night, he often appeared in dreams that co-mingled the hostility from our prior interactions with the terror I had felt on the day of the shooting. Kept locked away by day, the massive inventory of memories — my own and all those I had collected from others since — were irrepressible in sleep. There were variations on the theme, but one nightmare recurred more often than others, and always had the same ending:

I'm standing on the sidewalk outside the emergency room. There's all the commotion and chaos you'd expect in a war zone — screaming and shouting, anger and fear, sheer panic. I'm enveloped in a hazy cloud of impending doom, shut off from the rest of the world, unable to run away. How I've gotten there, I don't know. But I do know why I'm there, and I do know what will happen. Suddenly, the shooter is looming above and pointing his gun directly at me. He's menacing and mocking. He makes it clear he intends to kill. At first, I try to reason with him, but then begin to beg and plead, as the possibility of resolution quickly fades. But it's futile — there's nothing I can say or do to change the outcome we both know is coming. It's already been decided. It's irreversible. He tells me it's inevitable and that I can't stop him. He smiles knowingly. There's no escape, there's no hope. I scream and cover my face as he pulls the trigger. It's always the same.

The nightmares haunted me on many levels, but what I came to dread most about them was the feeling of pure hopelessness. Until then, I had taken hope for granted. There was always another day, another chance, another try. Hope was the motivation to get up eight times after falling down seven. Through these dreams, though, I learned that hope was also something I had not fully appreciated, until I had experienced its complete absence. Fortunately, the loss was transient, and hopefulness returned in daylight. But the process of losing it over and over in those dreams, and staring repeatedly into that void, was hellish.

The one variation in these dreams is the role in which I am cast. Sometimes, I am in Kelly's place; sometimes, Kelly has already been shot and I am the shooter's next target; sometimes, I am there to intervene on Kelly's behalf. Regardless of my role, for a split-second in every dream, I believe I can alter the ending. But that belief is always yanked harshly away and replaced with the stark, sudden knowledge that the shooter holds all the power.

On the day of the shooting, he did, in fact, have all the power. It wasn't hypothetical, or a figment of my imagination. It was a truth I had not wanted to accept. But we had not relinquished power that day — he had taken it from us. The challenge, though, was not to let him continue to keep that power, in a present in which he no longer existed.

***

Occasionally, the shooter also popped into view while I was wide awake. A mental image of him would be triggered whenever I came across his name in a document, or whenever I encountered someone with the same first name. But one time while walking through the basement hallway near the main pharmacy department, I came around a corner and was surprised to see him staring out to me through unblinking eyes, grinning from ear to ear, and surrounded by smiling co-workers.

He wasn't there alive and in person, of course but in a photo that had been newly hung on the wall. The tradition of displaying a group photo from each quarter's employee recognition ceremony had been established long ago, and framed collages of past years' honorees lined the long corridor.

I was stunned and confused — and instantly angry. I imagined yanking the large frame off the wall by myself, but I knew I couldn't because it was firmly attached to comply with the latest seismic regulations. I stomped furiously down the hallway toward the facilities department, to demand it be immediately removed.

The photo was included, I was told, because there were other winners in it, too, and it would have been unfair to them to exclude it from the display. Plus, its absence would leave a noticeable gap in that year's collage and disrupt the design of the exhibit, I'm informed, and they had held off as long as they could.

Needless to say, and less important to repeat the &%$#@ words I'd said in response, the group photo was removed shortly thereafter. I didn't care about the hole it would create; I didn't care about fairness. Well, I did care about fairness...fairness to Kelly and Hugo. I refused to have a photo of the murderer on any wall in our hospital, much less, in our Hall of Fame. And, in this nightmare, I did have the power to alter the outcome.

I learned later that the people who had initially hung the photo on the wall were new to the organization and unaware of the significance. Life had moved on, and, as more and more new employees joined the organization and the shooting remained unspeakable, the event had receded from the surface of everyday conversations.

One day about a year later, though, I came around that same corner and discovered the group photo had been returned to its place in the framed collage — but photoshopped into the shooter's place was the face of another employee! It was a clever solution, but unnerving and deeply unsettling, nonetheless. Doctoring the picture didn't change who I still saw in it every time I passed by. Instead, it silently spoke a thousand words about the complexity — and inescapability — of the trauma we had faced.

———◆———

"Nothing ever goes away until it teaches us what we need to know."

~ *Pema Chodron*

———◆———

Wolves in Sheep's Clothing

FOR THE NEXT SEVERAL YEARS, the organization experienced substantial growth and improvement. We expanded our footprint by building new outpatient facilities and formed new alliances and partnerships which broadened our market reach. We added new training and educational programs to strengthen our workforce and to reduce unemployment in the community. We continued to recruit top-notch clinical and leadership talent to round out our state-of-the-art services and deepen the bench. Many of us took on new leadership roles in regional healthcare policy groups, professional associations, and in local community service organizations. And we acquired a neighboring hospital on the brink of closure, which saved more than 600 jobs and kept an emergency room open that was vital to the residents on the east side of the city.

By all indications, the organization, as a whole, had healed and fully recovered. We hadn't returned to a pre-shooting baseline — in many ways we had surpassed it. Within a few short years our new team had hit its stride, and an air of optimism and enthusiasm permeated the organization. To suggest our workplace was kumbaya would be disingenuous — we had setbacks and failures, and there were cracks in our renewed unity, but overall, we'd rebounded stronger than ever. We had beaten the odds and spiraled upward after the trauma. I was proud of our team's — and my own — resolve to move forward and not allow it to divide us or hold us back.

But sadly, one-by-one, many of those who had been directly traumatized by the shooting began to leave. With each departure, there were a few sympathetic murmurs but little discussion. I began to wonder if I'd someday hear myself say, "And then there were none."

I was convinced, though, that I would never need to leave prematurely because I had successfully transitioned to leading us in the "new normal" while also actively addressing my own symptoms of post-traumatic stress along the way. I had never been more professionally fulfilled, nor more certain I was right where I belonged. I was in it for the long haul. And I believed the emotional wounds from the shooting could be completely healed by continuing to manifest the deep meaning I'd found in my work. Surely, the strong alignment of my own calling with the organization's mission would continue to propel me forward into the future.

But I was also privately tormented and haunted by a past that was ever-present. Though the shooting was rarely mentioned in public except at the anniversaries, I was well-aware of the underground rumblings and whisperings that lingered. Reminders of the shooting continued to pop up in a variety of unavoidable and surprising ways, often triggering an intense, internal storm of flashbacks and emotions.

It was impossible for me to avoid the physical landmarks of the shooting. Every time I passed the Outpatient Pharmacy while walking through the hospital lobby, I'd congratulate myself for not once having thought about the shooting. I did the same as I passed the Trauma Room, as I walked through the Emergency

Department, as I walked on the sidewalk near where Kelly had been shot, and as I passed the remembrance garden just outside my office — realizing, of course, that the shooting was the only thing I had been thinking about.

What I could avoid, though, was another layoff. Whenever we faced a budget crunch and were challenged to "Close the Gap" with a widespread reduction in force — which was almost every year — I shut it down. I had seen how threats of layoffs in the past had damaged morale, and how the stress and tension of job insecurity was an additional worrisome burden on employees who worked in an already intense and stressful environment.

The looming threat of layoffs was commonplace in our national work culture, and layoffs had become a widely accepted condition of employment — and managing them was a required competency for leaders. Undertaking a layoff was often framed as good stewardship, a badge of courage or bravery, or an example of a leader having to "do the hard thing." And yet, businesses lamented the fact that people weren't engaged and loyal, and wondered why the next generation was so prone to jumping from job to job.

I didn't have an explicit "No Layoff" policy and I didn't reject the idea that there were instances when they were necessary to ensure the economic survival of a company. I knew there might come a time we would need to invoke the WARN Act again and announce a company-wide layoff...if workload decreased substantially and was not expected to rebound, if patient volume plummeted, or if we lost a large contract, for example. But the new litmus test was whether I could stand up in front of employees and clearly explain why it was justified — and also commit to not taking a bonus in any year that downsizing became truly necessary.

Every year, though, we found a way to meet our financial goals without using a layoff to get there. We had become more cautious about hiring so that we wouldn't find ourselves overstaffed with permanent employees, and we improved our ability to flex and adjust to swings in the workload. We established a practice of retraining and redeploying people if we thought their current jobs were not going to be necessary in the future. We didn't guarantee employment; there were times when jobs had been eliminated, when programs lost their funding, when services were outsourced, or when mergers made a position redundant. And there were times people were let go for poor performance.

But we never used organization-wide layoffs as a "stick" to keep people motivated or to keep them from becoming complacent, or because "everyone else was doing it." I didn't believe that a little fear "kept people on their toes." We never again used it as a tactic to meet an aggressive productivity target, or to correct an overly optimistic budget, or to shore up investment interest losses in a fluctuating market, so that we could get a bonus. I wasn't going to repeat 2009.

While I did not believe that using layoffs as a routine method to achieve a budget was responsible leadership, I also knew that the word "layoff" was highly triggering for me; every time I heard it, I reflexively cringed and winced. For me, the word was associated with murder and tragedy.

It would be easy, then, to jump to the conclusion that my righteous avoidance of layoffs was rooted in a subconscious fear that executing another would result in another shooting. I have no doubt there was some kernel of truth in that, but in retrospect, the word also triggered something even more psychologically destructive than fear and superstition. It triggered shame. Shame in knowing that the layoff of 2009, in my opinion, had been unwarranted and unnecessary. Shame in not having the courage as the CEO to resist the directive, and to say, "No." Shame in following through with it anyway. And the shame of receiving a bonus in that same year.

* * *

It wasn't just reminders of 4/16 or the word *layoff* that relentlessly triggered me; breaking news reports of mass shootings in public places and workplaces did as well. From mid-2009 to late 2014, their frequency was alarming — Fort Hood, Hartford, Tucson, IHOP, Seal Beach, Oikos University, Aurora, Oak Creek, Minneapolis, Sandy Hook, Washington Navy Yard, Chardon High School, LAX, Fort Hood (again!), Overland Park, Isla Vista... and by the time you're reading this, the list has grown to epidemic proportions...

"Life is not measured by the breaths we take, but by the moments that take our breath away" took on new and sinister meaning. I learned to hate the sharp and stabbing, purely visceral feeling of surprise that was instantaneously evoked, and to dread the blunting numbness of grief and sadness that always followed. I knew that for the survivors, the trauma would continue to be felt long after the media coverage ended. The event might be over, but its impact was just beginning and would ripple out in ways they could not yet imagine. They had involuntarily joined a club no one knew existed prior to belonging to it.

And I hoped they were getting help because I knew how important professional help had been for me. I'd been seeing a therapist from the beginning, and her expertise had been invaluable in helping me to both explore my feelings and develop healthy coping strategies — and to address ones that were not beneficial. Much of our time, though, was consumed by all the unexpected complications that arose in the aftermath which, at the time I thought were preventing me from fully processing the original trauma. But now I think I also intuitively knew that as long as I remained in the organization, I could not admit and confront the feelings of shame that I'd kept deeply buried and hidden... from my therapist and from myself. And we both knew I had no intention of ever leaving.

On top of my internal conflicts and the myriad external triggers, dealing with new threats of violence to the organization further undermined my recovery. The sources and seriousness of the threats varied, but they were relentless. Every four to six months we'd be faced with a new one, and in the shadow of the trauma, it was hard to tell if the rate was trending upward, or if I was just now more aware and sensitive to them. In hindsight, it was both.

And though most threats turned out to be relatively minor — at least judged that way after the fact — several were all-hands-on-deck, full-blown crises.

***

"You have to decide, ma'am, whether or not you're going to evacuate the hospitals." A small group of us stood huddled on the street outside the emergency room and everyone looked to me for a response to the officer's request. We had just been told a message had been received stating a bomb had been planted at the medical center and that it was set to explode at 10 o'clock this morning. It was 8:45am.

The message had been left on a doctor's office voice mail late the night before but not discovered until staff arrived at work in the morning. We were told the message was brief and that the caller's tone had been measured and serious, but he had not ranted and raved. If not for the threat part, his anger might have been considered rational and reasonable. There were no outright clues to the caller's identity and no other details had been revealed. He had not identified a specific target or given a clear reason for planting a bomb. But more important to us at that moment, was that he had not disclosed its exact location.

The bomb squad had already been dispatched and began searching the campus. The plan was to start with the facility's life support structures and the most heavily trafficked common areas, and then to systematically sweep through the rest of the medical center. But there was a catch: with more than a million square feet of office and patient care space, it would take at least eight hours to thoroughly search the whole campus. With just over an hour until detonation, we had to consider evacuation.

"What's the likelihood that the bomb really exists?" I asked, wanting the officer to tell me we had nothing to worry about and that the sweep by the bomb squad was just basic protocol. It had been several years since the shooting, but the phrase "those who threaten don't act..." echoed in my mind once again, and I latched onto it with hopefulness. I wanted to believe it was a hoax.

While the answer was that it was rare for threats like this to be carried out, this one could not be dismissed based on low probability alone, they said, because the threat assessor had determined it was credible, and if the caller was telling the truth, the risk of extensive mortality was high.

There was another catch: although the police officers and threat assessor could provide advice and counsel, we were informed that since the medical center was on private property, the decision to evacuate, or not, was entirely up to us. At first, I was taken aback — what the hell?! I expected the authority of law enforcement to supersede ours, private property or not, when a threat of physical violence was involved. I expected them to take full command and to direct *us* on next steps. I pushed back. They must be passing the buck.

But as we went back and forth a bit, I realized I was wrong. It did make sense that the final decision had to be ours. Only we could assess the unique ramifications of evacuating all of the patients, staff, and visitors in our two acute care hospitals at the same time.

It was a dilemma unique to hospitals. We were not a typical business, in a typical office building filled with healthy people who could all exit to safety on their own and then stand outside to await the all-clear sign, or simply go home and return another day. In those settings, it was almost always wisest to evacuate when faced with a threat like this because even if it ended up being a hoax, there were no downsides other than some lost time or sales. But evacuating a hospital could have deadly consequences. It was an act of last resort... when no other option was available and when the benefits clearly outweighed the risks.

The inpatient facilities were large; the adult hospital had seven stories, the children's hospital had three, and in both hospitals, the ICUs were on the top floor. In total, more than 600 inpatients were inhouse, and nearly 100 of them were on ventilators in the intensive care units. Most of the rest of the patients weren't ambulatory either. Many were critically ill or under anesthesia in operating or procedure rooms or in active labor. All pediatric patients required adult supervision and could not evacuate on their own. Additionally, hundreds of patients and their families were being cared for in our outpatient facilities, clinics, and diagnostic centers that were spread across the campus. And there were easily more than a thousand staff members, physicians, and visitors on site.

In the past, we'd done small-scale evacuations of a unit or clinic in response to relatively minor issues — a power outage, heavy smoke, a chemical spill — and even in response to the discovery of a suspicious package. And though we'd practiced whole hospital evacuation during tabletop drills, we'd never had to do it for real on this scale. Evacuation of the entire population was a massive undertaking, and a decision to do so could not be taken lightly, especially in the absence of absolute certainty that a bomb existed.

We immediately convened our disaster response team and gathered in the Incident Command center. I needed the wisdom of the group and the answers to three big questions: One, how long would it take to safely evacuate everyone? According to the caller, we had just over an hour before the bomb detonated. Two, what were the specific consequences of moving a large number of seriously ill patients? And if we couldn't evacuate without injury, how many patients would be harmed in the process? And, three, was there even a safe place, presumably outside and far enough away from a possible bomb, to relocate all the patients? And could we adequately care for them outside, until the situation was resolved?

We quickly determined it would be impossible to safely evacuate both hospitals within the next hour. We estimated it would take at least eight, about the same amount of time as it would take to search for the alleged bomb. And we agreed it was highly likely the emergency evacuation process would result in casualty for a significant number of patients. We couldn't leave the seriously-ill ones behind, of course — without a doubt many might die or deteriorate if left alone without a caregiver. And, in answer to the third question, we couldn't identify a relocation site that was secure either. Though we had mobile tent hospitals that could be set up in the parking lots, we couldn't be sure the bomb hadn't been left in a vehicle parked in one of those lots.

Like in one of those ethics thought experiments, I had a difficult decision to make. The evacuation might save many, but the process would almost certainly result in harm to some. Conversely, I could avoid causing harm by not evacuating, but that choice could result in mass casualties if a bomb did, in fact, exist and exploded. Unbeknownst to most people, their fate was in my hands, though the ultimate outcome was not entirely in my control. Whether or not we evacuated, would not change whether, or not, a bomb existed.

Our foundational credo was "first, do no harm." That oath, combined with our evaluation that the risk of injury during evacuation was high, and the experts' assessment that the probability of a bomb existing and exploding was low, led to my decision to not evacuate. But that did not mean we had to sit idly by. Though we could not entirely control the outcome, we were not helpless or hopeless; we could direct our energy and resources toward minimizing injury in every other way possible.

We went on high alert — we diverted ambulances so that no new emergency patients arrived, cancelled the rest of the morning's elective surgeries and outpatient visits, and limited access into the medical center. We closed all the fire doors and deployed the management team to discreetly look for suspicious packages in their units and departments. Though a complete search would take more time than we had, we clung to the possibility that if a bomb existed, it could be found and diffused before it detonated. We sent out a carefully worded announcement to apprise our staff and visitors. We didn't want to overly alarm or to cause panic, or cause a stampede to the exits, but it was important to let people in on what was happening and the actions we were taking.

The remainder of the hour flew by — and the designated time came quickly rushing toward us. All conversation in the incident command room stopped as we paused to watch the clock on the wall. Logistically, we'd done all we could. As the clock ticked toward 10, we stood silent and still, as if we were collectively willing the bomb threat to be a hoax and praying it would all be okay if it weren't. I held my breath and listened in anticipation for an explosion in the distance, while bracing against the possibility it could be close by.

There was no explosion. A little cheer erupted in the command center and a palpable wave of relief passed through the room. It was over.

Not so fast, someone said — we could not be sure it was a hoax until the bomb squad had completed its sweep. And though we had to remain vigilant until then, we began to scale back the incident command team and gave the green light to return to normal operations. As each hour passed by without incident, the level of anxiety decreased, and feelings of safety were restored.

It was nearly 5pm before we received the all-clear sign. No explosive device or suspicious packages had been discovered. The day had begun early with a board meeting and ended by returning to business as usual — with a bomb threat in between. All in a day's work, we joked. To say we were giddy would be an exaggeration, but not by much. The relief was intoxicating.

But so was the kind of teamwork experienced in the throes of a life-threatening crisis. Once again, as a team, we had remained composed, performed in unison, and deliberately and methodically addressed the situation. We hadn't over-reacted, or under-reacted, emotionally or logistically. In many ways, the experience further strengthened the bonds between us and deepened the trust we had in one another.

In the end, the decision to not evacuate had been the right one. But as I think back on it all these years later, I realize it was the right one only because there hadn't been a bomb. If a bomb had been planted — and people had been hurt or killed when it detonated — we all would have quickly second-guessed the decision. We would have said how irresponsible it had been to not evacuate. The concern about causing injury during evacuation would have been discounted or minimized, in hindsight, and called overblown or insignificant. The very same decision — which was heralded as level-headed and rational — would have almost certainly been characterized as poor judgment and a colossal failure to react appropriately. It was a powerful example of how readily the quality of a decision is judged solely by the outcome.

Before adjourning for the evening, we conducted a quick debrief of lessons learned. Topping our list of improvements was the need to evolve the hospitals' evacuation plans to include the option of a partial evacuation. Though we could not have safely evacuated everyone in such a short amount of time, we could have evacuated ambulatory patients, visitors, office workers, and non-clinical staff — if we'd had a pre-developed unit-by-unit, floor-by-floor plan to guide us. We were accustomed to "triaging" patients into the facility; this scenario exposed the need for development of a more specific plan for triaging people out, too.

Though I was buoyed by the good feelings of relief and team unity, as I drove home that evening, the stress bubbled to the surface and I struggled to choke back tears. I'd become practiced in bottling up my emotions, but the anxiety and tension did not simply disappear once the event had been resolved. Even if I'd jokingly called it "all in a day's work," it wasn't normal to feel like I worked in a war zone. Or it shouldn't be.

The fear of another violent tragedy was never far from my mind, and the threat was a taunting reminder that there could be another. And another, and another. I began to think not if, but when. Intrusive thoughts and nightmares of what *might* happen became intertwined with those re-enacting what already had. The nagging, little voice that whispered, "It's not safe here," was difficult to contradict.

A real bomb had not existed or exploded, but the real threat of it left plenty of emotional shrapnel behind.

* * *

Thanksgiving weekend of 2013 brought the next significant, all-hands-on-deck threat of violence when a known gang leader threatened to kill members of our staff if his newborn daughter died in our care. She had been born with a terminal condition and was not expected to live more than a few weeks.

The baby had been born full-term and the diagnosis had come as a complete surprise to everyone. Even though there had been no pre-natal signs and symptoms, the father blamed us: the doctors, the nurses, and the "hospital." And though his anger and grief were understandable, the threat was not. Initial attempts to de-escalate did nothing to reassure the team that he wasn't intent on carrying out his threat. Nor did having security tell him that he had crossed the line. Instead he laughed and said he didn't have any intention of killing anyone *himself*, as though to imply a novitiate could do it as a rite of passage. Perhaps to earn his first teardrops? "Those who threaten don't act..." did not seem to apply here. It was the only time I'd ever heard the threat assessor say he was afraid.

At first it seemed obvious that we had two options: ban the father from the hospital or transfer the baby to another facility. But it wasn't that simple or straightforward. Though it was well within our right to do so, and might have even been possible to have the father detained by the police, the first option would keep him from his dying daughter and the baby's distraught mother, which would have further inflamed an already tense and dangerous situation. The latter wasn't medically advisable; the baby wasn't stable, and the risk of her dying during transport was very high. Neither choice eliminated the threat, and both were more likely to exacerbate it.

Like the bomb threat, we were again in the unique position of responding to what might happen, but evacuating the parent or the baby wasn't a good option. This time we didn't have to find the 'bomb.' We knew right where it was; we knew who it was. And while our efforts needed to be focused on diffusing it, we also needed to do everything possible to keep our staff safe from harm in the event it did explode. They were afraid — who wouldn't be?! — and wanted assurances we would keep them safe.

We implemented a partial lockdown of the children's hospital and mobilized a visible force of armed plainclothes and uniformed officers on the unit and throughout the campus. We moved the other patients and their families for their safety and sequestered the baby into one room of the NICU. The baby's family was required to provide a list of expected visitors, and each had to agree to be searched for weapons on entry. It was made clear that anyone who made a threat, or who was found with a weapon, would be permanently removed from the campus, regardless of relationship to the baby. All were reminded that hostility toward caregivers made it that much harder for them to perform at their best.

Despite the uniquely stressful circumstances, there were plenty of staff members willing to take the clinical assignment of caring for the baby. They were compassionate, highly skilled, experienced clinicians and accustomed to working in an emotionally-charged environment, but they weren't accustomed to being potential targets of threats. We redacted all the involved caregivers' names from the medical record, removed their names from their ID badges, and provided them escorts to and from the parking lot to protect them. I knew there wasn't anything we left unchecked, or anything we were unwilling to do to keep them safe. I hoped it would be enough.

Once the additional security and safety measures were put into place, there was not much more we could do, other than to closely monitor the situation and try to maintain a calm environment. But, unlike the bomb threat scenario, where time rushed quickly toward a pre-determined hour of detonation, time, in this case, moved excruciatingly slow. The initial intense flurry of activity turned into a long, suspenseful, nail-biting wait. For nearly a week we were trapped in a surreal existence... managing a tense, hostage-like situation, while, in parallel, continuing to operate the rest of the children's hospital and the entire adult hospital, as though it were business as usual.

This dichotomy extended to my emotions as well — teamwork highs competed with worry and helplessness. I felt like we were sitting ducks. There were many ups and downs and near boiling-over points as new developments emerged throughout the week.

Tempers flared and nerves began to fray as the days passed by. Like all the others, I'm sure, adrenaline kept me going all day long, and kept me awake through the short, sleepless nights. Day after day, we hoped for a miracle, while remaining prepared to defend ourselves if the baby's condition worsened, or if she died. It gave new breadth to how I'd previously thought of the phrase, "holding vigil."

After six days, the baby was, miraculously (and because of great medical care) stable enough to be transferred to a quaternary center capable of performing the extremely rare transplant she needed. It was the best outcome possible. New hope for the parents brought resolution for us all. The handful of people assembled in the incident command center let out a little cheer as the medivac helicopter lifted off at 9:30 in the evening, a week after Thanksgiving. I breathed a sigh of relief. But the weight of the week was not lifted.

We had created the best possible conditions to stabilize the situation and increase the baby's chances of survival, and our additional security measures had kept our staff safe in the meantime. But I had no doubt that if the baby had died, the father would have attempted to carry through on his threat. The father's mocking hostility and disregard for authority, which mimicked the shooter's, had re-triggered all my previous feelings of terror and powerlessness.

In my role, I assumed and willingly carried the weight of responsibility for others' safety. I didn't doubt we would do all we could to prevent an act of violence. But this latest threat was another sobering example that, while we could influence the outcome, it was not entirely within our control. Accepting that universal truth, theoretically, was easy — but, in the aftermath of the shooting, living with it was not. The fear of losing someone else, another colleague, another friend in an act of violence had grown unbearably heavy.

As I drove home late that evening, stress and fear came pouring out. This time I did cry. And the whispers, "It's not safe here," grew louder and louder and more difficult to ignore.

***

"RUN"

"NURSE"

"GUN"

The hairs on the back of my neck stood on end. I pressed the cell phone closer to my ear and asked the caller to repeat what she'd just told me. Maybe it was a bad connection. Maybe I had misunderstood. Had the chaplain's assistant really said that these three words had been found hanging on the prayer tree? In the hospital's chapel? Usually, visitors left well-wishes on the prayer tree: a note of hope and encouragement for a loved one who was sick, a salute to honor someone who had passed, or a few words to celebrate the newly-born or newly-healed. My mind swirled in a mixture of confusion and dread.

Her voice still shook as she began to retell the story, this time slowly and with more detail. "Some of the notes people write are short and general, some are long and very, very personal, but all are heartfelt and sentimental," she said, and added that it wasn't uncommon for a favorite poem, or an inspirational saying, or a meaningful line of scripture to also be included. She called them "offerings" and "little glimpses into the soul." The prayer tree was, at its base, a gangly arrangement of plain wooden sticks, but as these individual notes were added to it throughout the week, it was transformed into a spiritual work of art. Reverence and awe had replaced the shaking in her voice.

"Once a week, all the cards are removed from the tree," she continued, "and the pastoral care team joins together in a circle to bless them in a simple, but beautiful and sacred ceremony." I imagined the tree stripped of its leaves and left bare, but available once again to receive and support new ones — a continual cycle of sprouting and shedding, blossoming and harvesting, growing and detaching.

Her tone shifted again as she told me that about 80 prayer cards had been hung that week on the tree. As she'd gathered them together in preparation for this morning's ritual, three had stood out; the words written on them caught her by surprise. One had a single word, "GUN," written on it in large, bold capital letters that filled the entire card. Another had the word, "NURSE," written on it, and the third, the word, "RUN." All three appeared to have been printed with the same pen and in the same handwriting.

She'd immediately shown them to the team; no one else had ever seen anything like this either. The "message" was startling and unnerving. What did it mean? Was it a warning? Was it an imminent threat? Since each word had been written on a separate card, it wasn't clear if there was an intended order. Was a nurse the target? Or the threat? Or was it just a harmless (though crass and disturbing) prank? At the very least, all agreed it was an intrusion, a violation.

They'd already called security, who in turn had contacted the police and our on-call threat experts. There was no need to assemble the whole incident command team; at this point, there was no specific action to take. We would just have to wait for the results of the investigation and for advice from the violence prevention consultants before deciding on the next steps, if any. We talked for a few more minutes, mostly, I think, in the hope that the shock would subside. Before hanging up, we arranged to connect again in a couple of hours, unless new developments made it necessary to talk before then.

I was offsite at a conference at a local university but had found a private place to take her urgent call. As soon as the call ended, I burst into tears. In a way, I was surprised by their suddenness and that they'd sprung out uncontrollably; I'd never cried while in the midst of the other threats. During a crisis, I'd always been intensely focused on leading the team — there were strategies to develop, decisions to make, actions to direct — things to do. But this time, there was nothing for me to do, nothing to keep the tears at bay.

My tears weren't just triggered by fear and anxiety. Five years' worth of pent-up anger and frustration spilled out as I cried. The illusion of control — "if we take the right action, we can stop it from happening" — had long ago been shattered. And with each successive threat, the protective layers of denial — "it won't happen again" and "it can't happen here" — had been slowly stripped away. Uncertainty and unpredictability were part of life, but this latest threat in the chapel was over the top. Was no place sacred? Was no place safe?

After a few minutes, I wiped my eyes and blew my nose, took a bunch of deep breaths, and tried to focus on the present. I was about to be busy in a different way. In 15 minutes, I'd get up on stage in front of a hundred people to give a speech and then participate in a panel discussion about the future of healthcare.

I went into the restroom and splashed water on my tear-stained face and on, what I imagined, were my red, swollen eyes. The woman in the mirror, though, looked wan and flat. She stared back at me through hollow, vacant eyes. She seemed to be a long way away, distracted and withdrawn. I was determined to reach her and pull her firmly back to the here and now. I imagined the 'Slap, and "SNAP OUT OF IT!!"' scene in the movie, *Moonstruck*. "COME BACK!!" I silently screamed to break the spell. Before leaving, I reapplied mascara and lipstick to return the color to my face.

After the panel discussion was over, I called back in for the update as planned. The bottom-line result was that the investigation was inconclusive. No additional clues or facts had been discovered. The chapel was open 24/7 and, though there was CCTV to monitor the entrance, the prayer tree was not within view of the cameras. We would most likely never know who had left those three cards, or why, or if it had even been meant as a threat at all. On the one hand, I was relieved there were no further developments and that it had not escalated. But the mysteriousness of it was unsettling. The case was closed, but not resolved. Could I trust that it was "over?"

I didn't stay for the remainder of the conference, but I didn't go back to the hospital that day either. Instead, I drove straight home, crawled into bed fully clothed, and pulled the covers over my head. It was one of the few times I'd gotten home before sunset. It was the middle of the summer of 2014, and there was still a lot of light left in the day. But I was in a very dark place.

It hadn't been the scariest of situations. It hadn't lasted very long. It had not been an all-hands-on-deck full blown crisis. In fact, very few people ever knew anything about it. But for me, the cards were an augury of a fast-approaching breaking point.

The words printed on them might as well have been,

"NOT"

"SAFE"

"HERE"

***

In many ways, navigating through these threatening situations — and several others that I'm unable to share the details of — increased my confidence and ability to manage and lead through crisis and adversity. But these weren't natural disasters or accidents. These were threats by people intent on terrorizing or causing harm. The fragile sense of safety and security I'd worked so hard to re-establish in between threats, was re-shattered again and again, and after each re-traumatization, I found it harder and harder to regain equilibrium.

My symptoms had become too significant to suppress, and I could no longer deny I had PTSD. The stress effects of the trauma, which were not just "post" one event, but were compounded by the emergence of new threats of violence and by the chronic exposure to reminders of the original shooting, had begun to take a heavy toll on my health. I was locked in a vicious cycle and spiraling quickly downward. And for the first time, I began to question my longevity in the organization.

"The changes we dread most may contain our salvation."

~ Barbara Kingsolver

An Assisted Fall to the Floor

I DISCOVERED FIRST-HAND you can't always accurately gauge the stigma of a condition by how easily it's tossed around or flippantly referenced in casual conversation, but rather by the responses — and looks on people's faces — when you admit to having it. Especially when it's classified as a mental health disorder in the psychiatric diagnostic manual.

Though "PTSD" is commonly used by the public, the condition behind it has long been plagued by myth and misunderstanding. It's invisible, can't be definitively diagnosed via a lab test or a brain scan, and is saddled with the stereotype that people develop it because they're weak or not resilient enough. I'm hopeful, though, that as more of us come out of the shadows to openly describe our experiences with PTSD, and as the research evolves, progress will continue to be made toward better understanding the underlying neurobiological injury, identifying risk factors, and dispelling the myths about PTSD that stubbornly persist.

Looking back at what had transpired at the time of the original shooting, its antecedents, and all that had happened in the five and a half years since, I wasn't surprised when I was diagnosed with PTSD. It didn't make it any easier to accept though. I was well-aware of the cultural biases surrounding

PTSD — and battled my own negative perceptions and self-judgment about it, too. For a long time, I had vacillated between emphatically reassuring myself I was okay, and cautiously floating trial balloons to those around me to let them know that I wasn't... hoping that I wouldn't be judged, that someone would understand, that I wouldn't have to give up the job I loved.

As a direct result of the trauma, my relationships with others were deeper and closer, and more than ever before, I appreciated and cultivated connectedness. I had a loving family and a supportive circle of friends, and I was highly visible and fully engaged in a vibrant and dynamic community. But even though I was surrounded by a lot of people I loved and cared about, and who I knew loved and cared about me — even though I *belonged* — I'd become more and more isolated as the years passed.

The circumstances surrounding the trauma and the stigma of PTSD had fostered a profound sense of separateness between me and others. Early on, the unspeakableness of the shooting created distance and kindled the development of PTSD; later, the unspeakableness of my struggle with PTSD further amplified and compounded the distance I felt. Before long, the trio of unspeakableness, PTSD, and separateness had become locked together in a self-perpetuating feedback loop, each continuously reinforcing the others.

I wasn't a secretive person by nature, but outside of therapy I had initially avoided talking about the shooting because of how shaky and tense I felt when I did, and how uncomfortable I sensed the topic made others feel. At first, avoiding it had been easier; rarely did someone else in my professional or social network ever bring it up. But I started to notice how often it was seeping into my conversations, and, how, as much as I'd wanted to avoid the topic, the one who almost always brought it up was *me*.

When the topic did eventually surface in a conversation, sometimes the other person said they'd steered clear of it because they didn't want to remind me of the event — as if they thought I'd forgotten about it or it had slipped my mind. "It's never NOT on my mind!" I silently screamed in exasperation. It made me realize, though, how many times in the past I, too, had avoided bringing up someone else's painful memory or loss — for the same reason. I didn't want to upset them to be sure, but I knew I also used this reasoning as an excuse to avoid my own discomfort when confronted with someone else's pain and grief.

Sometimes I'd receive advice that felt simplistic and reductionist, a la, *"Be positive, look on the bright side,"* or *"You're so strong, you can put that behind you,"* or *"You can't live in fear,"* or *"Bad things happen,"* or *"It could have been worse."* I knew people cared and the words were good-intentioned, but they often landed as one-dimensional and dismissive. I didn't lack gratitude. I didn't lack fortitude. I didn't lack positive thinking. I didn't lack strength. I didn't need pithy platitudes. But it also made me realize how many times in the past I'd offered similar words to salve another's emotional wounds. How I'd felt compelled to pacify, or distract, or change the subject to something pleasant and uplifting. How I'd sometimes resorted to using logic or facts to argue with their feelings. I'd told myself I was trying to help, and that my sage advice would motivate them to move on. Until I was on the other side of those words, I hadn't really understood that sometimes people who are suffering don't need to be fixed; sometimes, they simply need to be heard. And how much those words can piss you off.

Most people in my inner circle did listen patiently and lovingly — and often said they couldn't imagine what I felt. Sometimes when I heard the words, "I can't imagine," I'd zealously seize the opportunity to elaborate and over-explain, because I desperately *wanted* them to imagine it, as if that were the key to understanding. But I often felt as though I were speaking a foreign language — it didn't matter how many, or which, words I used, I wasn't going to be understood.

Many times, though, I ended up speaking haltingly or rambling on, trying to find just the right words to express my emotions about the shooting and to describe my struggle with chronic traumatic stress in a way that would convince them *why* I felt the way I did — while not over-sharing. But by the end of the conversation (usually a monologue), I almost always felt like I'd revealed too much and was too exposed. And still not understood. In frustration, I'd swear to myself that I'd never bring the subject up again, only to repeatedly discover that suppressing it, or avoiding it, was futile.

It would take a long time and, ironically, more distance to gain the objectivity and insight to know that the lack of understanding wasn't anyone's fault. Years later I came across this quote attributed to Jerry Lewis, which perfectly captured the impasse I'd felt at the time: "For those who understand, no explanation is necessary; for those who do not, no explanation is possible."

Sometimes the subject, though, was not raised by me at all but surfaced in completely unrelated circumstances. A few times a year, the local paper or a business journal would reach out for an update on the hospitals' performance or to interview me about what it was like to lead a large, complex organization in a notoriously thin margin, high-risk industry. "What's the most challenging situation you've led through?" and "What keeps you up at night?" were commonly asked — and innocently lobbed — questions. There were lots of good answers for both but only one authentic answer to each. I steered clear from responding with "4/16" and "fear of the next threat of violence," though, and answered instead with the business challenges and dilemmas that were expected and acceptable. That weren't unspeakable.

As much as I'd breathe a sigh of relief to have successfully sidestepped the topic, I was always left feeling as if it had been a missed opportunity to talk about the trauma and share lessons learned... and mistakes made. We couldn't be the only organization facing threats of violence, and we certainly wouldn't be the last to experience an active shooter tragedy. I knew it could be valuable for others to hear how it had uniquely impacted our organization and how it had changed me as a leader.

But even many years later, it was still too raw and sensitive a topic to bring into the open. It felt like I'd be tearing off the scab and opening a can of worms of unresolved conflict. I'd tell myself that next year I'll be able to talk about it; but another year would pass, and, still, it would be too soon. I began to wonder if it were always going to be too soon.

I knew keeping my diagnosis with PTSD a secret widened the separation between me and others. I felt the financial strain of remaining "off the grid." In order to maintain my privacy, I'd sought care outside our network of providers and did not submit the bills to our self-insured plan for reimbursement. I wanted to believe, though, that I could "come out," and I fantasized that sharing my struggle as a leader with PTSD might change viewpoints and help others. On the occasions when I carefully tested the waters, it was clear that doing so carried social and professional consequences — not only for me as an individual and for my career, but also for the organization. I had not developed PTSD as a result of an accident or from a trauma that had occurred elsewhere; coming out would inevitably mean revisiting the source of the blame, guilt, and shame that I felt — the layoff — which in the workplace, was even more unspeakable than the shooting itself.

It was a very different kind of softball question that eventually led me to come out at work, if only fleetingly. In the Fall of 2014, a few weeks after the incident in the chapel with the prayer tree, I sat down with my boss to review my performance during the past year and to discuss my goals for the upcoming one. As part of this annual process, each leader was also asked to commit to goals related to their personal health and well-being, in addition to the traditional financial, clinical quality, and strategic ones. Usually, we identified things like eating healthier, exercising more, taking up a new hobby, and walking 10,000 steps a day.

As we got close to wrapping up the meeting, I was asked what my own health goals were for the new fiscal year. Up until that point, the conversation had been light and easy-going, and the mood upbeat, bordering on giddy, because we were celebrating the close of an outstanding year. I hesitated. I could, once again, respond with an answer that I knew was expected and acceptable. But the part of me that no longer wanted to remain hidden and separate, that desperately wanted to *close the gap* of a very different kind, took over.

"Right now, what I'm most concerned about, is my mental health," I said. I was no longer smiling, and I looked away as I said the words "mental health." My tone had changed from light and breezy, to heavy and somber. After a moment, I turned to look her squarely in the face, and, as our eyes met, her head cocked to one side and her brow crinkled quizzically. Neither of us said anything. We just stared at one another, paused at the intersection of serious and kidding. Was I brave enough to follow through and say what I'd meant, or would I shrug and laugh it off, and return to celebration? And career safety? Maybe it wasn't too late to snatch my words back and replace them with "I'll take the 10,000 steps, please."

"I have PTSD." The words simply spilled out. It didn't feel like I'd made a choice to say them. It felt more like they could no longer be contained.

"I'm getting help, but…" was all that I added, and my voice trailed off as I saw from the look of surprise on her face that I'd already said too much.

"Oooooh, well, we won't be writing *that* down!" she responded, and immediately looked away. I knew her response was not because she did not care. In fact, I knew she cared about me a lot; apparently, so much so, that it was important to keep what I'd told her a secret.

"You're in your early 50s, aren't you?" she said, quickly redirecting the conversation.

I nodded. I'd just turned 51.

"Have you had your colonoscopy yet? How about the shingles vaccination?" she asked, clearly in search of something more acceptable than PTSD.

I shook my head "no."

"Well, how about we put those down, then, as your health goals for the coming year?"

I nodded in agreement and watched as she handwrote the words "colonoscopy" and "shingles" on my performance review in big, flowing script with a determined finality, as if to signal the matter was settled, the conversation was over, and there'd not be any more mention of the unspeakable.

The exchange had been brief, but the message was clear: I was good at my job and neither of us wanted me to lose it. But I could not come out with what was widely considered a mental health disorder and keep it.

With that now behind us, our smiles returned. Mine was not entirely a façade, but I knew I'd flashed it to camouflage the despair and disappointment I felt. Attempting to rebound and end on a high note, we spent the next few minutes once again congratulating each other for a great year and enthusiastically talking about the one ahead. We warmly hugged goodbye. We never discussed it again until it was too late. But in hindsight, it had already been too late.

***

For years, I passed this sign every morning on my way out the door, and again when I came back home at night. In principle, I couldn't have agreed with it more, but lately I'd started questioning if it was right. Was worry and the fear at its root, an illusion... the result of my imagination gone awry? Or was it the product of experiences I could no longer deny? Because what now seemed imaginary and invented, was the safety and security I'd long taken for granted. I had previously assumed the figure on the sign was dancing and twirling — floating free from the weight of worry. Recently, I'd begun to wonder if she were instead, slipping and falling — overcome by the burden of reality.

***

Logic told me we weren't in any more danger than we had been before the shooting, and I was convinced we were doing everything within our control to keep people safe and to prevent violence in the workplace. I downplayed the risk and tried to placate myself with facts and statistics. I reminded myself how well we'd managed each new threat and that nothing catastrophic had happened again. I didn't believe another tragedy was imminent, but I could no longer discount the possibility or quell the worry that accompanied it.

When viewed through the lens of trauma, the past had become prologue and disproportionately influenced my projections of the future. Being haunted by an ever-present past isolated me from others and being afraid of what *might* happen kept me trapped in an almost constant state of hypervigilance.

For five and a half years, I'd been on high alert and on guard, braced in anticipation of the unexpected. While my mind worked overtime trying to convince me that I was safe, my body stubbornly disagreed. "Fight or flight — or freeze" was my baseline now, and the chronic infusion of adrenaline and cortisol had left me anxious and uneasy, tense and taut. And eventually, completely exhausted.

I'd believed I could remain in the organization and overcome PTSD. Leaving was not only a pejorative — synonymous to quitting or giving up — it was also associated with excruciating, panic-inducing feelings of loss — loss of purpose, of belonging, and of my identity. Leaving equated with dying.

But staying equated with it now, too.

I was gridlocked in a lethal binary — I couldn't leave, and I couldn't stay — the solution was unimaginable.

The tipping point, though, came on a single day, in a single moment in early October 2014.

***

Every year, our health system convened a day-long meeting to celebrate the year's achievements, unveil new strategies for expansion and development, and generally inspire the entire 500-member leadership team. Traditionally, the president presented the "state of the health system," the treasurer summarized the annual financial results, and each hospital CEO presented a "leader of the year" award and introduced a video that highlighted their team's accomplishments and "proud moments."

The event was held at an offsite venue, central to all the facilities in our health system. It was a general-purpose theater with a large stage and a main seating section, both of which were elevated four feet or so above an empty orchestra pit that separated the two areas by about ten feet. The seating section had been set up dinner theater style, with long, rectangular tables arranged perpendicular to the stage. Though the configuration was convenient for note-taking or small group conversation, it made it difficult to see the speakers unless you turned your seat or body to face the stage. To compensate, the presentation slides were projected onto large screens positioned above the stage.

That particular year, the long-time leader of a survey and analytics company we'd worked with for years was invited to keynote the final speech of the day. He was a notable expert in employee engagement and had a reputation as an outstanding motivational speaker. As one of the speakers of the day myself, I had the opportunity to sit next to him at a table at the front of the room. He was funny and friendly and instantly likeable, and I'd enjoyed getting to know him a little bit as we interacted throughout the day. As the day went on, I grew more and more excited to hear his insights and ideas — and I knew we were in for an entertaining and memorable speech.

But even though most people were still in attendance when our guest speaker was introduced, it seemed the energy in the room had begun to wane. It was after lunch and late in the day and people were probably tired from craning their necks to see the stage. And since he wouldn't be using slides or other visual props, there was no need to watch the screens overhead. Instead, many appeared distracted by their devices or laptops, most likely multi-tasking, or trying to stay connected with their staff back at the hospitals and clinics.

But once he began speaking, it became apparent that it would not be necessary to focus on him visually in order to absorb his whole message. His rich, booming voice alone, which rose and fell dramatically, quickly commanded the audience's full listening attention.

From my seat at the front, though, I had an unobstructed view of him on stage. I watched as he began to pace, slowly at first, and to swing and wave his arms, moving in rhythm to the tone and tempo of his words.

But then his pace quickened, and I felt my body tense and stiffen. Despite his uplifting message, I prickled in apprehension as he began to stride back and forth across the stage.

One of the side effects of hypervigilance, I'd discovered, was that I witnessed many more accidents and mishaps — and people falling down — than I ever had before. When you're constantly scanning your surroundings, always on the lookout for danger, you tend to see things that you'd, otherwise, be blissfully oblivious to.

With each sweeping pass, the speaker crept closer and closer to the edge of the stage and the four-foot-plus drop to the hard floor below. I told myself not to worry — he was an experienced speaker and must be aware of the hazards of performing on a stage: the bright, blinding lights, the unmarked edge, the darkness beyond. And, the risk of becoming so engrossed in your own story that you could easily lose track of where you were.

Barely breathing, I stared intensely at him, riveted on his every step, trying to estimate the trajectory of his path, and willing him away from the edge. I took a shallow breath and mentally sighed in relief each time he stopped just shy of it and pivoted in the opposite direction. I'm not sure I heard a word he said, but I can still hear the sound of his shoes marching across the stage.

This went on for at least ten more nerve-wracking minutes. Didn't he realize how close he was to the edge? Couldn't he see that he was inches away? Should I call out to warn him?

Nope, don't do it, cautioned the pragmatic voice inside my head. My watchfulness was unnecessary. My worries were exaggerated and inflated. Imaginary, it added.

I quickly glanced around — no one else seemed even mildly concerned. My instincts must be faulty and abnormal. It was ridiculous to think he'd fall off the stage, the voice chastised. Of course, he knew what he was doing. And if I were to yell out to him, I'd be seen as nervous and anxious — and tightly-wound (which I was!). Instead, I kept my worry to myself and suppressed the urge to call out and alert him of the danger I so acutely felt.

But then suddenly, he tumbled soundlessly off the stage and plunged headfirst into the orchestra pit below. It happened so quickly that he hadn't even been able to break his fall. But to me, time slowed as he stepped off that stage, and, frame by frame, I watched as he fell. His face and shoulder hit the ground first. But then, as if defying gravity, he rolled upward and seemed to pause for a moment, upside down, on his head. I cringed at the awkward, neck-bending pirouette that followed, and gasped as his body tipped over and landed, breathtakingly hard, flat on his back.

I jumped up and ran to him before most knew he had fallen. Fortunately, there were many physicians in the audience, and several, who were close by, quickly made their way through the crowd of confused onlookers. For a long minute, the speaker lay on the ground. He was conscious, but, at first, he didn't move. I couldn't believe he hadn't broken his neck, given the way he'd fallen. But after another moment, he sat up on his own and leaned against the front wall of the stage.

Once the initial shock wore off, he insisted on getting back up to his feet and was adamant about finishing his speech.

The audience applauded his effort and tenacity, but after a few minutes back up on stage, he stopped, and said he thought it was best to take the doctors' advice to call it a day and get a further evaluation of his condition. We applauded his willingness to recognize that enough was enough, and that it was more important for him to stop and get the care he needed.

Surprisingly, he ended up not being seriously injured. Just some bruises and soreness, but no broken bones or dislocations. It had been a close call. But I also knew that if he had been severely hurt, it would have been hard to forgive myself for second-guessing and not trusting my instincts. I replayed the scene in my mind, editing it for an alternative ending, wishing I had called out to warn him of the encroaching edge, and prevented him from falling.

But I also considered the repercussions of this different ending, too. Calling out would have prevented a fall that no one else, including the speaker, had been concerned about or thought was likely, in the first place. No one in that room had shared my degree of alarm, so shouting out to him from the audience would have exposed my hypervigilance to all, at a time when I already felt the need to hide any indications that I was struggling with PTSD. I knew my vigilance was excessive — and becoming more so. In this instance, it hadn't been mistaken, but my recognition of it forced me to admit the extent to which hypervigilance was dominating my life. And the toll it had taken trying to keep it — and my other symptoms of PTSD — discreetly managed and contained.

In the scheme of things, this event was minor; it wasn't violent, or threatening, or in any way terrorizing. But his literal fall had revealed my figurative one.

***

All these years later, I think about how hospitals go to great lengths to identify patients at high risk for falling and implement measures to prevent or reduce their occurrence. And, how, if a patient does begin to fall, the staff is specially trained to gently assist them to the floor to minimize injury. In a lot of ways, that's what my family and personal healthcare team did for me. And though falling hadn't been a choice, staying down until I recuperated was.

I think we all thought a couple of months away on medical leave would be enough, but it didn't take long to realize that it wouldn't be healthy for me to return. Without relief from constant reminders of the past and freedom from ongoing threats of another tragedy, I would not be able to fully heal and return to a healthy baseline. I had recovered and grown as much as I could in a workplace that, for me, was both healing and harmful.

As I began to accept that I needed to leave the organization, I wrestled with so many contradictory feelings: I was angry and sad and devastated, and yet relieved and grateful and at peace, all at the same time. I was scared at the uncertainty of what lay ahead, and yet I had faith that it would all work out okay. I struggled with thoughts that I was abandoning my team, but I was also proud of how high-functioning and incredibly talented they were, and I knew that there were several who could assume my role and take the organization to the next level. In my heart, I knew that I had not stayed one day too long, nor was I leaving one day too early. I knew I was making the only decision possible. Not just for me, but for everyone else too. The organization deserved a healthy CEO, and I deserved to recover.

And while I had been open with my bosses and my senior team about my reasons for leaving, crafting a message that communicated my resignation to the rest of the organization and to the community at large, was trickier. As much as the unspeakableness of the trauma had sown the seeds for my unwellness, speaking about it now, on my way out, would not be helpful or constructive.

Even if I could not be completely transparent with everyone and publicly share my true reason behind my leaving, I could ensure my departure didn't cause further harm or hardship — to myself or for the organization. I hoped, though, that there would come a day when I could speak out about it in a way that was helpful to others.

In the end, I said my goodbyes as plainly as I could, and with as little mystery as possible, while not re-opening the wound for any of us:

> Dear colleagues ~
>
> First of all I want to thank you for the tremendous outpouring of personal cards, letters, and calls to me over the past several months with regard, initially, to the announcement of my medical leave and subsequently to the announcement that I would not be able to return to my role as CEO of the three best hospitals in the greater Long Beach region. It has been truly inspiring, touching and heartwarming to have so many of you reach out with love, compassion and concern. It is heartbreaking to me to not be well enough to return to a job I considered my calling, and to an organization, team and community that I love.
>
> I do very clearly want to also reassure you that I am slowly recovering and am not suffering from cancer or a terminal illness. I am sorry if my relative silence has

naturally led to worries such as that. And I'm profoundly grateful that my privacy surrounding my health issues has been maintained and respected.

Lastly, I want to take a moment to let you know how incredibly honored and privileged I have felt to have spent literally half of my life in a remarkable and outstanding organization — remarkable because of the people who comprise it, and outstanding in its razor-sharp focus on the mission of serving the healthcare needs of our communities. I could not be prouder to have spent my entire professional career with an organization that has served those needs for more than a century, with a steadfast goal of providing the highest quality care possible...while always stretching to do even better with each patient encounter.

Several years ago, a vision statement was created to describe the essence and philosophy of how we each serve as leaders in the work we do. I share it with you because it was deeply meaningful to me personally and also became a kind of "mantra" that helped me on my healing path over the past several months:

"We are a team that, as a whole, is greater than the sum of our parts. We are a team in which the very best of each is shared, the very best of each is nurtured and the very best of each is expected. Each of us fully embraces the responsibility and the privilege of stewardship and courageous leadership, and our actions reflect the values of accountability, best practices, compassion and synergy. We are a team whose talents and strengths are fully expressed and whose members are deeply

connected to the mission and the legacy of the organization. We know and believe that what we do, and who we are, make a profound difference in the lives of others."

I am incredibly fortunate to have been able to learn and grow within a supportive and forward-thinking environment. Every day I reflect, with an almost overwhelming sense of gratefulness, in the fact that I got to be part of it all with you! I have great admiration and respect for each and every one of you. I cherish the many life-long relationships that we've developed and that I know will continue well into the future.

I'll close now with one of my favorite sayings from the wise Dr. Seuss: "Don't cry because it's over; smile because it happened."

With love,

Diana

"The curious thing about quests is that the seeker embarks on a journey to find what he wants, and discovers, along the way, what he needs."

~ *Wally Lamb*
(The Hour I First Believed)

PART

4 Compassion

T HE FIRST CLUE that perhaps I had not chosen the right place for refuge occurred before I'd even stepped foot onsite. I had the distinct impression that the escorts from Ridgeview who greeted me at the airport baggage claim were assessing me, rather than simply transporting me. It had seemed odd that two had shown up for a task that only required one. Though outwardly friendly, they weren't focused on small-talk or pleasantries; conversation, it seemed, was a vehicle, a means to an end for evaluating my level of cooperation and compliance. As they placed my suitcase and my carry-on bags in the trunk of the shuttle van, they asked for permission to inspect them for "contraband" when we arrived. I knew I wasn't booked for a month as a guest in a high-end spa or resort, but this felt unnecessary, a bit melodramatic. I laughed, thinking they were joking. They didn't really need to search *my* belongings. Of course, I wouldn't bring something illegal or dangerous! It hadn't occurred to me that I wouldn't be taken solely at my word, but from the stern looks on their faces, I knew their inquiry was non-negotiable and that the only acceptable answer was consent; clearly, I'd not read the fine print on the pre-admission agreement. So, I said, "Yes," to the search of my belongings; I certainly didn't have anything to hide. The request was disconcerting and off-putting, but I was looking forward to being there, so I quashed the little voice that wondered whether I was making a mistake, the little voice that began to ask if I knew what I was getting myself into.

We left the airport and drove through and then out of town in relative silence. In the 30 minutes or so that passed, I was left to contemplate how I'd gotten to the point where coming here seemed to be my best option for recovery. Months before, I'd fallen, metaphorically, off the stage and left the cast of a play that had run most of my adult life. When I left the organization, I believed I'd hit my lowest point and could only bounce back up from there. But, with the cover of busyness gone, nothing stood between me and the sadness I'd tried so long to hold at bay. An abyss called depression had opened up beneath me and I hung suspended above it, with free-fall all but imminent.

Of all the aspects of PTSD, the two most debilitating for me were isolation and hypervigilance. Ironically, what I thought would cure the hypervigilance — leaving the organization — had resulted in me feeling even more isolated. My tethers to purpose and belonging had been all but severed, and I struggled with the fresh grief I felt from loss of my identity. And though I was now free from the daily exposure to landmarks which reminded me of 4/16, my news feed continued to be bombarded with reports of more horrific shootings across the country: Marysville Pilchuck High School, Rosemary Anderson High School, Montgomery County, Waco, Charleston Mother Emmanuel Church, Chattanooga Mall, Lafayette movie theater, Umpqua Community College, and Colorado Springs. When would it end? (We all now know the answer to that question.)

I had retreated, but not far enough away to escape the horrors of the outside world, nor for long enough to successfully confront the demons of my inner one. I'd been getting regular care from a terrific team of trauma specialists, but together we recognized that I was getting worse, not better. And then two things happened, one not long after the other, that finally convinced me I needed to do something different: one was a text from my terrified daughter, telling me that her school was on lockdown because of an active shooter outside. After a harrowing hour, we were notified that no shots had been fired, the police had apprehended the perpetrator, and no one at the school had directly been in danger. But it sent me down a path of panic and unleashed a flood of flashbacks that took days to recuperate from. The second was the final straw: the mass shooting in San Bernardino — which was in a healthcare facility not far from my home, and in a place where employees had been killed by their co-workers.

I couldn't keep spinning and churning. My world was collapsing in on me. I needed more intensive care, and I needed to retreat farther, I'd thought, to a safe harbor where I could curl up, cry it out, and then process it all from a clear, unobstructed viewpoint. I'd lived with this story for so long; maybe I'd benefit from the objectivity of strangers. I imagined I would go away and return magically renewed and restored. Re-set. The spell of the past would be broken, and I'd be ready to reclaim my life and move forward.

Now as I rode in silence, a state and a time zone away from my family, my caregivers, and my closest friends, I began to think that maybe retreating — *running away* was how it was beginning to feel from this distance — was only going to be more isolating.

The shuttle van slowed as we turned off the highway, onto a long and winding, dusty paved road, and into the middle of nowhere. Eventually we passed through a security gate — was it to keep people out, I wondered, or in? — and entered a rustic, southwestern ranch-style compound of beige buildings that seemed to be right out of the mid-1970s. Little stucco and brick one-story buildings dotted the grounds that were well-kept and nicely manicured and landscaped with mature trees and cacti of all sizes. Not quite an oasis, but a pleasant looking desert *sanitarium*, I thought wistfully, as the expression, "careful what you wish for" simultaneously came to mind.

I was escorted (sans my suitcase and carry-on bags) to the empty lobby where I sat for nearly an hour, waiting and wondering what would happen next. Where was everyone? Was I early for check-in? What was the hold-up? Weren't they prepared for my arrival? I hadn't slept well the night before (or, for that matter, the more than 2,000 nights since 4/16) and felt the irritable beginnings of a head cold. I just wanted to be shown to my room and to sleep. And at a thousand dollars a day out-of-pocket because I had an HMO that didn't cover this facility, what was left of my curiosity crept toward impatience.

Finally, an older, nicely dressed woman came into the lobby and I turned expectantly toward her. Her face lit up when she saw me, and she made a beeline right over to greet me.

"You must be the new patient! We're so glad you're here!" Her warmth and friendliness melted the annoyance I felt about having to wait so long. In a very loud voice, which seemed unnecessary since there were only two of us in the room, she told me all about the facilities: the gym, the pool, the walking trails, and the wonderful group here. But then she leaned in closer to me, her eyes darted nervously around the room as if checking to see if anyone was watching, and she whispered conspiratorially that everyone here was crazy. *Crazy!* she repeated, while miming its universal sign with her hand. The wild look in her eyes removed any doubts about her seriousness.

Up to that point, I'd mistakenly thought she was an employee. She was a patient, I realized. I mentally corrected myself; she was a patient, *too*. I was also a patient. I was not an attendee, or a retreatant, or a guest. I was in my element — I was in a healthcare facility — but I was here in an unfamiliar, and increasingly uncomfortable role.

She waved enthusiastically goodbye to me, and as she turned to leave the room, I saw that she was wearing slippers. I hadn't noticed them before. It would be an exaggeration to say that she had shuffled off in them, but it would more honestly reflect the snarky level of judgment I felt about our encounter. It wouldn't be the last time during the course of my stay that I blushed with dual embarrassment – embarrassment at the ease in which stereotypes and stigmas came instantly to my mind, and embarrassment for being here myself.

After a little while longer, another woman came into the lobby and asked me to follow her. This time I looked for a badge to confirm that she was a staff member. She led me into a smaller room and began the registration process, initially collecting the typical demographic information and then proceeding down a long list of questions about my past medical history, before finally delving into the reason for my current admission.

Didn't they already have that information on file? I had given it all to them in advance of my arrival, and I'd had multiple conversations by phone with the admissions personnel to confirm receipt. My doctors had been in contact with them to discuss my medical records and had provided a thorough history of my diagnosis of PTSD. Hadn't they read their own notes? Why was I having to repeat it all? Was she asking because they didn't know or because she wanted me to confirm what had been provided? I kept all these questions to myself, though, because as an administrator, I did understand that it was all just a routine part of the admission process.

My frustration with the process increased though, as we approached the sixty-minute mark. It sure was taking a long time to reconvey the information I'd already provided. That was before all the forms were produced for me to review and sign — Advance Directives and Patients' Bill of Rights and insurance coverage (or lack thereof) and patient financial responsibility and limits of their liability and treatment disclaimers and HIPAA compliance. I wanted to complain, but I didn't; I understood the hospital's process, but now I understood it from a patient's perspective.

Once all the standard forms were signed, the intake nurse then moved on to a "coping" checklist, focusing primarily on a long list of ones that could be harmful: in short, though, did I use drugs, alcohol, or cutting to cope? Did I have an eating disorder? Other addictions? Had I ever thought of suicide? I didn't really think anything about or object to the line of questioning; I was clinically depressed, so the questions were not in any way unexpected or unreasonable. I was completely forthcoming: yes, sometimes I used alcohol to take the edge off. *Who didn't* was what I thought and said so out loud. I didn't use street drugs or narcotics, but I admitted I'd recently tried marijuana; it didn't work even though I desperately wished it had, I added. I didn't have an eating disorder, but I elaborated on the two times in the past few years when I'd purposely withheld food, speculating that it might have been because subconsciously it was the one thing in my world I'd felt I had complete control over. Regarding addictions, if I'd had one, I said, it had been to work, but I'd stopped that cold turkey months before. And, lastly, no, I wasn't suicidal, but sometimes I did just wish I could simply disappear.

She smiled knowingly, sympathetically even, to all my responses, which at the time had seemed as crisp and concise as what I transcribed above, but in retrospect were rambling — and maybe, just maybe, a smidge defensive. As she systematically entered the data into the computer between us, I saw that she was checking a lot of the boxes but leaving out the qualifiers I'd offered. Qualifiers that could have easily sounded like denial, I suppose, to someone who'd heard it all before.

With the verbal part of the admission process complete, she said she'd do a physical exam next and added that my clothes would be searched for contraband, and that I was also required to consent to urine and blood tests to make sure that I was clean. If cleared, I'd be admitted to the residential program; if not, then I'd be admitted to detox.

"What? Whoa," I said. "There must be some mistake."

I wasn't here for rehab. I wasn't addicted to drugs or alcohol before or now. Again, she smiled, knowingly and sympathetically, but this time I heard her think, "Everyone who comes here says that at first."

The battery of tests for illicit substances and alcohol all came back negative. I felt vindicated, but also strangely relieved, even though I'd known it was the only outcome possible. It was like the relief you feel when a police cruiser, with its lights flashing and siren blaring, comes rushing up behind the car you're driving, but then, thankfully, zooms on past. You're relieved you're not being pulled over, even though you know you haven't been speeding, even though you know your tags are up-to-date, even though you know your taillights aren't out. Even though you know you signaled when you changed lanes a mile back.

After the intake process was finally complete, my suitcase and carry-on bags were returned to me (sans my cell phone that I learned was contraband), and I was led to the nurses' station where I was presented with a little paper cup of medications for me to take before bed. The only prescription drug I took regularly was an antidepressant. I looked in the cup; it looked as though there were five or six different pills and capsules in it, none of which looked immediately familiar. I balked and asked why I was being prescribed any medications. I was told they were standard orders for most new patients. But I didn't even have a treatment plan yet, I protested, and I hadn't been seen by a physician either. (As it turned out, I wouldn't be seen by one until the third day.)

It didn't seem right to be given drugs without explanation, so I asked to see the medication orders, which seemed to catch them by surprise. I was concerned when I saw the list of drugs; a couple of them had the potential for significant side effects and could be powerfully sedating, especially when taken in combination, and especially, for someone unaccustomed to them. I told the them that I didn't want to start taking all these new medications without more discussion about why, and without consulting my doctor at home. There were two, however, on the list — an antihistamine and melatonin — that I did agree to take because my cold had gotten much worse over the course of the day, and I thought they'd ease my symptoms and help me sleep. The caregivers in the nurses' station were friendly and seemed understanding, but I could tell it was unusual for a patient to pick and choose which medications they would take.

I didn't reveal that I'd been a pharmacist and a hospital administrator in my former life; I was here as a patient. I didn't want to double-check or second-guess; I wanted to be taken care of. And I didn't want to seem resistant or difficult, I wanted to cooperate — I wanted to be a good patient. I had a whole new appreciation though for what that meant, now that I was the patient in an environment that was familiar to me, but also began to feel strangely upside down.

I washed the two drugs down with a large glass of "sleepy time" tea that I'd also been handed, knowing full well that the doses were walloping and might make me feel loopy and woozy. But I figured I'd go right to bed, and when I woke up in the morning, I'd be a little more rested and my cold would be better. I'd sort out the confusion tomorrow, I thought, and reminded myself that I wanted to be here.

By then it was around nine o'clock in the evening. It was the middle of winter on a moonless night; the air was cold and the sky pitch black. I was shown to my shared room in one of the little buildings on the outskirts of the compound. My roommate was already asleep. I wondered if she was the same woman whom I'd met in the lobby earlier in the afternoon. I crept in, trying to not disturb her. I didn't unpack anything but quickly changed my clothes and crawled into bed, and before long, I fell into a deep, stuporous sleep.

Suddenly, I was startled by a whoosh of cold air and a bright beam of light in my eyes. I didn't know what was happening, and, for a moment, I wasn't exactly sure who or where I was. I struggled to get my bearings. Through squinting eyes, I peeked toward the commotion and saw a woman bundled in a heavy coat, standing in the open doorway and waving a flashlight across the dark room. She said something to me that I didn't understand. My dazed mind couldn't catch up to her words. But, then, just as suddenly as she'd arrived, she was gone. I would have sworn it was a strange dream — and chocked it up to fever and too much cold medicine — if it hadn't happened at least two more times before morning.

I woke early with a terrible sore throat and headache. My congestion had worsened, and it hurt to take a deep breath. The room was icy cold. I'd forgotten to turn on the heater, not realizing how cold the desert is in the winter.

My roommate was still asleep. I wasn't sure what time it was. I hadn't brought a clock and didn't have a watch. It was still dark, but the clear sky was beginning to brighten. I put on my clothes and splashed water on my face, and then left the room and walked back over to the building that housed the nurses' station, intent on complaining. What possible reason would there be for someone to barge, unannounced, into my room, not just once, but several times throughout the night? In a croaky, shrill voice, I declared that I'd come here to avoid being surprised and startled.

In response, I heard the dreaded words, "you have to understand." I was told it was protocol, that the "bed checks" were required to ensure the safety of the patients. Every patient room was monitored every two hours throughout the night, regardless of why the patient was there, regardless if it was inconsistent with an individual patient's needs or preferences, regardless if it were contraindicated for their diagnosis. It was a standard, universal practice for all patients. I was given ear plugs and an eye mask and was told that they would ask the attendants to check more quietly the next night, in hopes that I wouldn't be as disturbed by the intrusion. They said if that didn't work, they'd give me a sleeping pill (??!!) so that I could sleep through.

The ironic thing was that I did understand their side of things. I did understand their processes and reasoning. And I thought back to all the times in the past when I'd received similar complaints from patients about noise and their sleep being interrupted. In particular, I thought of their complaints about the timing — 5am — of the daily blood draws. Patients described being startled awake when the privacy curtain between their bed and the next was flung noisily open, and without warning, the bright fluorescent overbed lights were flipped on. From the hospital's perspective, there were lots of good reasons for obtaining blood samples in the very early morning. Sometimes, a fasting result was needed. Sometimes lab results were precursors to additional tests, exams, and treatments, and often, they yielded important information for morning rounds. The routine was key to launching and organizing the day's workflow. And, it was how "we'd always done it."

I now remembered how I'd listened sympathetically to patients' complaints, but often responded with some long explanation to justify our process. I'd reassure them that, next time, the caregivers would try to tiptoe in and gently move the curtains so that they wouldn't be disturbed more than necessary. Now I knew, though, how it had probably felt from their point of view, and how my version of "you have to understand" must have landed. I had gone from the corner office of a hospital, to being in the bed of one. And the view from one was considerably different than the other.

**

The next two days were a blur as I tried to acclimate to my surroundings. I was taken on a tour of the grounds and soon realized just how small 35 acres could feel. I was introduced to most of the other patients and began to participate in the scheduled activities and group meetings. But my head cold had moved into my chest, too, and I now had full-on laryngitis. I struggled to say even a few words without provoking a long coughing spell.

There were lots of rules and little privacy. I was not imprisoned but was not free to venture offsite either. The vibe was a lot like summer camp, but with a hint of *Orange Is the New Black*. I didn't see how I fit in, and I wondered when the PTSD program would begin.

On the third day, I finally had my first appointment with a physician. It was appalling to me that it had taken so long. But surely things would get sorted out now. Following brief introductions, he asked me why I was there. I couldn't tell if he asked because he wanted me to explain it in my own words, or if he truly didn't know. Based on my encounters with others over the past couple of days, I was beginning to think no one knew why I was here ... or, they thought I was here for a different reason.

When my doctors and I had begun searching for a suitable place for me to go for PTSD treatment, we discovered that, although there were a few stand-alone programs for veterans, there were none geared toward civilians. Of the many residential treatment centers that claimed to have a specific PTSD program, all were connected in some way to a rehab facility. And though I didn't need that kind of care, there were many aspects of these facilities that we thought might be helpful anyway — they were quiet, secluded, and safe — and they advertised access to trauma-informed professionals.

We narrowed the list down to a handful of accredited organizations, and after several consultative conversations, we picked the one that convinced us its PTSD program was separate and distinct from a typical substance abuse recovery program. They'd also reassured us that I'd be in a cohort with others who were also struggling with PTSD. From what I'd experienced so far, the former was not true, and the latter had not yet happened. I was beginning to doubt it would.

I was a bit wary, then, when he asked why I was there. I told him I had developed PTSD following a shooting at the hospital where I'd worked, and that I'd been the CEO at the time. I kept my description of the event short and didn't elaborate on the details of 4/16, or thereafter, but said that feeling responsible was at the core of my struggle.

"You know that's irrational, don't you?" he interrupted when I said the word "responsible."

I *knew* it was considered irrational, I said, but *feeling* it, wasn't, I argued. I explained that being responsible was foundational to my definition of leadership, and a lifetime of training and experience had instilled the belief that it was an essential characteristic of a good leader. Being responsible was an expectation that I'd had of myself, and one which was constantly reinforced by society's messaging. Long before the shooting, I'd echoed the drumbeat: "Good leaders take responsibility!" "The buck stops here!" But after the shooting, being "responsible" was my Gordian knot.

I thought that if he viewed my situation through that prism and filtered it through the extenuating circumstances leading up to, and occurring after the shooting, he might understand why I said I'd felt responsible. If he'd been in my shoes, might he, too, have felt similarly?

Instead, we went down a rabbit hole, splitting hairs over definitions. I was cranky and sick, and, frankly, tired of trying to find just the right words so that someone else here would understand something I didn't yet completely understand myself. The conversation devolved into a debate about PTSD, and he eventually summed it up by saying everyone handled trauma differently, depending upon their past histories, personalities, level of resilience, etc., and that not everyone who went through trauma developed PTSD. Because, some people, he added, handled shock better and were able to adjust more easily to adversity and hardship. He didn't exactly drip with empathy or respond with understanding.

There wasn't much written about PTSD that I hadn't consumed in my search for answers and resolution. Most studies estimated that 3 to 20 percent of people who had been traumatized met the criteria for a diagnosis of PTSD, but prevalence varied widely by group (e.g. active military and veterans, civilians, children and adolescents) and by the type of trauma they'd survived (e.g. combat, mass shootings, natural disasters, sexual assault) (Kilpatrick, 2013). It was unclear if lack of access to healthcare, delayed onset of symptoms, or an unwillingness to report due to stigma had affected the rates, as few studies directly addressed those factors. But the good news was that not everyone who experienced trauma developed PTSD. And, since most people didn't, the obvious question, of course, was why some did.

To explain why, much of the research had focused on identifying pre-existing conditions (e.g. previous trauma, history of abuse, mental illness), on assessing pre-event mindset and resilience, and on determining if there were genetic differences between those who developed PTSD following a traumatic event, and those who did not. And while all of these were legitimate and important factors to consider, newer studies had suggested the ones that may be more strongly correlated to an increased risk, were those describing the traumatic event itself (e.g. severity, suddenness, unpredictability, human-caused, occurring in a place where safety had been reasonably assumed) and those describing the individual's connection to it (proximity, relationship to perpetrator or victims, moral conflict, as examples) (Kilpatrick, 2013). Cutting-edge work had also been published which focused on the neurobiological changes that can be caused by trauma and the physical effects in the brain and body (van der Kolk, 2015).

The point of my digression now…is that by the time I arrived at the treatment center, the field of PTSD study had come a long way, even though there were still many unanswered questions. Though the term "PTSD" had been used colloquially as a catch-all to describe difficulty after any kind of trauma or adversity, the etiology for an official diagnosis was significantly narrower and only included exposure to death, threatened death, actual or threatened serious injury, or actual or threatened sexual violence. So, it surprised me greatly to hear him overgeneralize the diagnosis, and I bristled at his conflation of trauma with adversity and hardship.

More alarm bells rang when I was told that the medications that had been prescribed for me on admission were the "gold standard" for PTSD. There was no medication gold standard for patients with PTSD, and the drugs on the list were mostly sedating, anxiolytic, detox meds. When I said I wouldn't take them unless he consulted with my physician at home first, he said that if what I had been doing at home had worked, I wouldn't have needed to come here, and added that healthcare professionals, like me, were usually the most resistant to care because they thought they knew better and weren't patient with the "process."

I'd come here because they'd touted their PTSD program. I'd been led to believe that I would be with other patients who had PTSD, and that the clinicians here were experts in PTSD. I was not an expert in the scientific or therapeutic field of PTSD, but I was expert in my own experience with PTSD. I'd researched my diagnosis, tried to be well-informed about the latest treatment modalities, and wanted to participate in decisions about my care, but so far, I'd had felt unheard and discounted by many I'd encountered here. It was very different from my experience with my caregivers at home. For the first time, I felt the vulnerability of being at the mercy of a healthcare system. It was eye-opening and discouraging and gave me new appreciation for why "patient-centered" care was so important.

It was clear they had no specific treatment program for PTSD. It was a traditional rehab facility, pretty much a one-size-fits-all kind of place, and all patients were viewed through the lens of addiction. When you're a hammer, everything looks like a nail, as they say. Most people were here for 30 days to dry out or detox; some had come voluntarily, some were court-ordered. Most were repeat visitors. For some of their families, it was the penultimate straw; for others, the camel's back had been broken long before. On the harsh side, it seemed to function more as a temporary holding place, and with a revolving door and a less than 15% success rate, it was hard not to conclude it was a money-making mill. I do not belong here, in this kind of place, I'd thought at the time.

But, on the more generous side, most of the staff members and clinicians were kind and wanted to help, and the facility had a lot of amenities for respite and relaxation. The other patients I'd met were friendly and considerate. I was already here (and I'd already paid for it), so I might as well make the most of it. I admit I was curious, too, about the whole thing. I decided to try to settle in, and thought I'd stay a few more days — at least long enough to get over my cold before I traveled back home.

I got into a daily rhythm of walking and writing, joined in on a few more groups, and listened to a lot of other patient's stories and shared my own. It didn't take long until I assimilated into the little enclosed community. And, soon, a few days turned into a couple of weeks.

**

As I began writing about this first part of my stay at Ridgeview, I wondered if I would be brave enough to include it in this memoir. When I returned home, I'd sheepishly shared the experience with my immediate family and closest friends and had spent many hours downloading and debriefing with my therapist, but it was not something I felt very comfortable disclosing, much less discussing with anyone else. I didn't really like to think about it all that much either. For a long time, I was embarrassed I'd been duped, embarrassed I'd misunderstood what I was getting myself into, and embarrassed that I'd been there in the first place. I'd just wanted to put it behind me and forget it ever happened.

In the end, I decided to include it with the hope it would serve as a caveat to other patients who are in search of a place to go for intensive PTSD care and respite, and that it might motivate other treatment centers to develop more specialized programs. Unfortunately, they will be needed as the number of people struggling with PTSD grows — especially, as shootings in public settings with war-grade assault weapons continue to occur.

I also decided to include it because, while being there had taught me a lot about what it was like to be a patient, I'd learned so much more about myself as a human being. I was confronted with the shallowness of my knowledge about addiction and mental illness, and I came face-to-face with my prejudices and negative preconceptions about people who had ended up there. I learned that I had a lot in common with almost everyone there: each was suffering, each felt they'd come to the end of their rope, each had felt the sharp pain and devastating consequences of loss, and, with rare exception, each was trying to find him or herself. Maybe they'd do so on this admission, maybe it would take more, but most wanted to recover. Who was I to judge? It was humbling to admit that the assumptions I'd made were often faulty and sometimes unkind. But doing so, deepened my capacity for compassion toward others, and in the process, toward myself.

And, lastly, there was another reason to include it: as disappointing as it had been to be in a place that was not ideally suited for a patient with PTSD, it ended up being the turning point in my own recovery.

I had gone there to find what I wanted, but along the way, discovered, instead, what I really needed.

―――◆―――

"The great stillness in these landscapes that once made me restless, seeps into me day by day, and with it the unreasonable feeling that I have found what I was searching for without ever having discovered what it was."

~ Peter Matthiessen
(The Tree Where Man Was Born)

―――◆―――

14 Rescue

D URING MY STAY AT RIDGEVIEW, I befriended a donkey named Rosie. She was one of a dozen or so rescue horses and donkeys who lived in the stables on the property. I spent hours brushing her coat and mucking her stall and, through the facility's equine therapy program, learned about the unique prey/predator relationship we have with donkeys. They're naturally afraid of us, but we're naturally respectful of their size (and their hooves and teeth). As herd animals, they're exquisitely attuned to our emotions and body language, and the key to successfully working with them is by establishing mutual trust. You can't just pull and prod to get them to do your bidding, and yanking on a donkey's reins just makes you both frustrated. I learned the best way to lead Rosie down a difficult, twisty, rocky, dusty trail was to calmly walk alongside her, gently coaxing, but with a firm hold on the reins so that she didn't wander off to nibble on the brush.

One day, a stable hand shared a fable with me about an old farm donkey who had fallen into a deep pit. As hard as she tried, the donkey was unable to climb the steep sides and escape from the pit on her own. After a while, the farmer came along and discovered her plight. From the edge of the pit, the farmer started hooting and hollering at the donkey, thinking that might scare her out. But that didn't work; the donkey was now just more confused and afraid. The farmer then tossed a rope down and lassoed it around the donkey's neck, thinking he'd be able to pull her out. He pulled and pulled, but the donkey stubbornly resisted. Maybe he could motivate her to scramble up the sides by throwing rocks at her, he thought. But that just made the donkey mad, and she started braying loudly. Finally, the farmer tried to lure her out with apples and hay. No matter what the farmer did, or how hard he tried, the donkey wouldn't budge. After a long day, both were exhausted.

The next day, the farmer tried all these things again, but still the donkey was stuck. He lost all hope that he'd ever be able to get her out. From the look in her sad eyes, it seemed she felt the same. It was obvious that the pit was a hazard, so the farmer decided to fill it in so that none of the other farm animals would fall in and suffer the same fate as the donkey. Unfortunately, the donkey would then be buried in the pit. The farmer was heart-broken, but he didn't see any other solution. He soon got to work, shoveling dirt into the pit. At first the donkey was dumfounded by what was happening, and then bereft when she realized that she was being buried alive. As the farmer shoveled, the dirt began to accumulate on her back. But then unexpectedly, the donkey shook it off her back and began tamping the dirt down into the bottom of the pit with her hooves. With each new shovelful, the ground beneath her rose up a little more. Eventually, the pit was filled in, and the donkey walked right on out. She was free.

This simple story profoundly shaped the rest of my stay at Ridgeview. I was there for retreat, hoping to escape the outside world, but it dawned on me that I'd also come here expecting to be rescued from the bottom of the deep emotional pit I'd fallen into. While I needed assistance and could not do it alone, no one else could rescue me. I had to rescue myself.

My perspective on recovery shifted — I did not have any further to fall, and it was time to shake the dirt off and take charge of my own salvation. It was time to reclaim a sense of belonging and purpose, and to begin to move forward. I accepted that the process would unfold step-by-step, each sequentially making space for and facilitating the next. Rosie, the donkey, was symbolic of that inflection point — and I still have a framed photo of her in my home to remind me of it.

***

My job had been a predominant source of fulfillment and happiness, and I felt lost without it. Many have said that happiness is found, not by "having what you want," but rather by "wanting what you have." So, with this in mind, I began by making a list of all that I was grateful for in life. It turned out to be very long, and nowhere on it was a title or an accomplishment or an achievement. It was filled mostly with gratitude for people, but also for the good fortune of having a nice home, financial security, and a stable community to live and raise my children in. At the top of the list was my inner circle of family and friends. I might have lost one tribe, but I still belonged to another, more important, and the people in it had been there all along. I wasn't really lost after all.

I saw more clearly the chasm that had grown between us in the years since the trauma. Oddly, retreating to Ridgeview and being physically far away made me aware of how emotionally distant and unavailable I'd been to the members of my family, even when I'd been physically present. I hadn't fully appreciated either just how much the shooting, the threatening events in the aftermath, and my increasingly obvious PTSD symptoms had stressed each of them, too. I wasn't the only one in my tribe who was suffering. I wasn't the only one who needed support and care. While reconnecting with those I dearly loved and who dearly loved me was key to my healing, it was key to theirs, too. More than ever before, I realized how much we needed one another.

With a rekindled sense of belonging, I began to think about my purpose in life in a new way, too. In the past, I'd mostly equated my life's purpose with vocation, and because I'd believed my career was over, I'd spun aimlessly and adrift for months. Even so, I realized that I did still have an important purpose — two interdependent ones, actually — the health and well-being of my family and becoming whole again myself.

For the first time in months, I was beginning to believe that I would fully recover and started thinking about the prospect of finding new purpose professionally, too. Just because I no longer worked in an organization with a deeply meaningful mission, didn't mean there weren't countless other ways for me to find meaning in work again. I wasn't ready to completely retire, and my career had not ended; it had paused. While I knew I might not choose to return to the same kind of work, I now knew that nothing stood between me and discovering a new calling.

Moving forward wasn't entirely contingent on my ability to sidestep or eliminate obstacles in the path ahead. There were aspects of the past that would hold me back if I didn't confront and resolve them. Or more accurately, there were aspects of the *trauma* that needed to be confronted and resolved, so that the trauma could be put in the past, where it belonged.

Each time I told my story to the other patients and clinicians at Ridgeview, I noticed more and more anger bubbling to the surface, often eclipsing my sadness and grief. Like a lot of people, I preferred to avoid anger or bury it away. And to never show it. I thought anger was undignified and unpleasant. Unbecoming.

Unacceptable. Un-leaderlike. And I'd had a lifetime of practice with locking it away in an imaginary iron-clad chest and attempting to throw away the key.

I'd had 14 nights of solid sleep — the eye mask and ear plugs had worked, after all — and was finally over my cold. I felt so much better physically than I had in a long time and was beginning to bounce back emotionally. It seemed fitting then, in this serene and calm environment, to confront the anger I felt about the shooting that clearly still existed despite years of trying to bury or deflect it.

Uncensored, it didn't take long for me to draft a very long list of things about the shooting I was angry about. Afterwards, I spent a few days thinking and writing about each of the items on the list, and interestingly, the feeling of anger associated with almost all of them began to dissipate and disappear in the process. Most, I realized, were old news now, and few had much impact, in reality, on my current life.

In reviewing the list, there was a noticeable and shocking absence…the shooter's name. It was inconceivable to me, bizarre, even, that his name was omitted from a list in which he should have been at the top. When I thought about the shooter though, I found it hard to feel any anger toward him at all. I felt nothing, as though a vacuum existed around my memory of him. This bothered me. How could I be angry about a bunch of petty things, but feel numb about him? Then I realized that, while his name was not on the list, mine was.

By killing himself, he had not had to answer for his actions, and in his absence, a gigantic void had been created. When there's a void, I've learned, it's often filled in with a narrative that can be both untrue in fact and, yet, resoundingly plausible to the storyteller.

I thought back at my defensiveness with the physician who, earlier in my stay, had challenged me when I'd said I felt responsible. I'd wanted him to understand why I felt that way, but we'd spent all our time arguing about whether my thoughts and feelings were irrational or not. In the context of the setting we were in, the word "irrational" had landed on my ears as a substitute for "crazy."

In order to let go of my belief about being responsible, I didn't need to be convinced that I was irrational — my logic and reasoning were not flawed — I needed, instead, to be convinced that my belief was just plain and unequivocally wrong. I needed to know, and to believe, that no matter what the shooter's reasons or motives had been, I was not responsible for his actions. And I was not responsible for why it had happened. And though I had said those words to myself before (as had a few others), it was not until that sobering moment — when I saw my name on the list, but his was egregiously missing — that I truly believed it.

* * *

Mohini was a rare white tiger who, in the 1950s, lived at the National Zoo in Washington D.C. Confined for years in a twelve-by-twelve-foot cage, with iron bars and a cement floor, she spent her days restlessly and ceaselessly pacing its perimeter. Realizing that she was not thriving, zoologists created a larger, more natural environment for her and were excited to finally be able to release her from the cramped enclosure. Freed at last, they expected her to bounce and leap joyfully through the expansive habitat. But instead, Mohini retreated to one small corner and continued to pace a twelve-by-twelve-foot path, her freedom forever limited by bars which no longer existed. Sadly, she remained for the rest of her life in that one small corner and never ventured beyond an imaginary boundary of her own making.

In coming to Ridgeview, I had retreated to a little corner of the world and, initially, continued mentally pacing the perimeter of a space I'd been trapped in for years. If I remained confined, it would be in a cage of my own making.

It was time to go home and leave the narrative of being responsible behind.

**

I'd learned a lot of lessons while away at Ridgeview, and I'd also found my "voice" again, too. Not only had the laryngitis I'd arrived with resolved, but I'd spoken up about what I needed and had resisted the pressure to conform to things that I knew weren't right for me. I never did take those medications and found out later that the physician never consulted with my caregivers at home while I was there. I was bothered by that and by some of the other things that I'd experienced and witnessed while I was a patient there. It didn't seem right that I'd been misled about the attributes of the program in the first place. A treatment plan had been cobbled together for me while I was there, but it was not the comprehensive PTSD program I had been promised.

A couple weeks after I returned home, my doctor, therapists, and I each called and wrote to the facility's administration to register our concerns, hoping they'd either develop a true program for patients with PTSD or stop advertising that they had one. A month or so later, all claims related to having a distinct PTSD program were removed from their website.

I was glad about the outcome at the time, but I have conflicting feelings about it now. I would have never chosen to go there if I had known their claims were not correct, but then I would have missed out on so much that I'd learned there. I had found answers to questions I hadn't anticipated, met goals I didn't know I had, and was stretched beyond boundaries I didn't know existed.

But the single most valuable outcome from my time away occurred as a result of two separate long-distance phone calls I had with my therapists back home. At the time, I'd been unable to label or precisely describe what had transpired, but I was well-aware of their transformational impact. Though the outcome didn't have a name, it had sparked a profound and lasting change in me. I knew I had found what I was searching for, even though I had not yet discovered what it was.

Like so many of my experiences stemming directly and indirectly from the trauma, I was finally able to identify it by writing about these two conversations. In doing so, I reconnected with the peaceful and soothing state of transcendence I'd felt at the time, and a deep and soulful knowing began to emerge. I realized that I'd been trying to name something that could not be grasped or clung to. It could not be attained as a result of an order given or a proclamation made. It could not be demanded or achieved through force of will. It was something that could only be freely given and willingly accepted. It could only be invited in, welcomed, and embraced. It was an act of love. And it was essential for healing and recovery.

It was forgiveness.

———◆———

"If you must look back, do so forgivingly.

If you must look forward, do so prayerfully.

However, the wisest thing you can do, is to be in the present.

In the present, gratefully."

~ *Maya Angelou*

———◆———

CHAPTER 15   Rebound

"**R**EMEMBER, DIANA, BREAKDOWNS lead to breakthroughs!" I once had a mentor who was fond of this saying, and although I'd experienced its truth repeatedly through the years, in the context of recovery, its wisdom and utility resonated with me more than ever before. I was pretty sure he hadn't had nervous breakdowns in mind, I thought with amusement, but it was no less true. And though it doesn't do full justice to all the soul-searching, the hard, physical work, and the emotionally grueling re-processing that facilitated many of the breakthroughs in the year and a half following mine, the upshot was that I was well on my way to rebound.

It was the spring of 2017 and I'd been invited to give the Commencement address at my pharmacy school alma mater. I was healthy again, so the timing was perfect. Like the graduates, I was entering a new phase of life as I re-launched my career, so coming full circle and returning to where it had first begun, seemed especially apropos.

Over the years, I'd been frequently asked to speak with groups of students to share what I had learned as my career progressed from student to CEO. While the students always appreciated words of encouragement and inspiration, rarely did they want to be lectured to about management theory, or to have a laundry list of competencies, skills, or to-dos regurgitated at them by an outside speaker. Mostly, they wanted mentoring, career advice, and to glean pearls of wisdom from real-life stories.

Though I steered clear of direct references to the trauma in these kinds of talks and substituted other stories in its place, it always loomed large and was never far from my mind. Privately, I knew it was either the primary source of, or had strongly reinforced, almost all of the most important lessons I had learned about leadership and life. It was impossible for me to disregard or deny its impact and influence, even if I could not yet openly declare it.

To prepare for the Commencement speech, I went back to my notes and my collection of stories and lessons learned to mine them for the kind of guidance that I thought would be most pertinent and helpful for new grads on the brink of their careers. I ended up sharing most of the key takeaways I'd selected with the graduates, but some were left out because they would have stretched my 10-minute allotment to an inadvisable 45 and would have broken one of the rules for ceremonial addresses which was affectionately known as the "3 Bs: Be bold, Be benevolent, and Be gone.

Whether they made the final cut for the graduation speech or not, I soon realized that several were applicable and useful for me, too, as I began the process of commencing once again. It would be wise for me to not simply dispense advice but to take my own as well.

***

It's surprising how close you are to the action when you sit at field level at a Major League Baseball game. For many years

I had the opportunity to regularly attend Los Angeles Angels' home games with close friends whose season ticket seats were a few rows behind the Angels dugout, half-way between home plate and third base and thrillingly close to the action. The foul balls that sailed into our section — usually deflected off the bats of left-handed hitters — were frequent reminders of just how close we were to that action. Fortunately, most of the balls that came our way had grazed the bat and were popped up high into the air, which gave us plenty of time to redirect our attention from our conversations and concessions and try to catch them.

Based on my confidence as a long-time athlete (though weekend warrior was more accurate by then), I believed it was impossible to get hit by a foul ball — as long as I was paying attention. I was in control of the outcome: ideally, I'd be able to catch it — or at the very least, I could duck out of its way. Based on my experience at these games, that had always been true. I hadn't caught very many balls, but I certainly had never been hit by one either.

About a year and half after the shooting, I went to a night game against the Seattle Mariners. It was an exciting game with a lot of action on and off the field — lots of scoring and lots of foul balls — a lot to pay attention to. At the top of the 9th inning, the Angels were leading 7 to 3, and, with two pretty quick strikeouts, it seemed a win was in the bag. But then a single was hit to left field, a walk followed that, and another single brought the runner home from second base. The score was 7 to 4 with a runner still in scoring position. The nervous excitement of a certain win turned into nervous apprehension, as the lead was now in real danger of disappearing.

Especially, since Ichiro Suzuki was up to bat next. We hoped he would be the last batter, but we knew he would be a tough final out. He was one of the greatest hitters of all time and known for getting his bat on nearly every pitched ball which so many times before had resulted in a base hit. It also meant he hit a lot of foul balls — and, as a left-hander, those foul balls often flew into the stands on the 3rd base side of the field.

To face the great Ichiro and save the win, the Angels brought in their ace reliever, who was fresh from the pen and had an overpowering 99+ mph fast ball that most batters could only fan at as it blew by. When the first two pitches to Ichiro were strikes — one called, and the other, an uncharacteristic swing and a miss — the tension in the stadium eased a tiny bit. He was down to his last strike. As was tradition, the entire crowd rose to its feet to cheer for the third strike and the final out. But the next two pitches just missed the strike zone and the count went to 2 and 2. Our uneasiness returned.

Like everyone else in the stadium, all my attention was focused on the pitching mound and home plate. I held my breath as the pitcher unloaded another blistering fast ball. Ichiro took a full hard swing at it and this time he connected with it, but instead of the ball being sent toward the outfield fences, it ricocheted off the bat at an almost perfect 90-degree-angle and came screaming our way. Everyone nearby shrieked in surprise and jumped to the sides to get out of its way. Instinctively, I knew that the low flying line drive was coming too hard and too fast to be caught with my bare hands. My only choice was to get out of the way, too. Or try to.

In the split second it took for the ball to reach me, all I could do was turn my back and twist away, hoping it would miss me. But the ball hit me squarely on the butt — and the force of it was stunning. It knocked me off my feet, and pain instantly radiated across my entire backside. I hung — draped over my seatback — with my butt and feet in the air and my head in the row behind me, for what seemed like a very long time, though it was hardly a minute.

My first thought was amazement: I had no idea getting hit in the butt by a ball could hurt so much. My second, was disbelief: I had not believed it was possible for me to get hit by a ball. I'd been paying attention and hadn't looked away for a second. And my third, was vanity: I hoped they wouldn't show the replay (and my butt) on the jumbotron.

Once people around me realized I'd been hit, they rushed toward me to help me back to my feet. I wasn't too eager to sit back down, of course, but I didn't have to: there was still one more strike before the game was over. Fortunately, that came quickly with one more pitch, though Ichiro did get his bat on the ball; thankfully, it grounded out to the infield. (I didn't see it, but that's what I've been told.) The game ended with a "W."

As we began to leave the stands and head for the exits, my last thought was more practical: I wondered where the ball that hit me had ended up. Shouldn't I at least get to keep it as a souvenir? But it was nowhere to be found — my friends say it hit me so hard that it bounced back onto the field. I'm sorry now I hadn't had the wherewithal to ask the usher to retrieve it at the time — and to get it autographed by the great Ichiro. I could have kept the ball in an acrylic box alongside a commemorative photo of the bruise it had left (with the stitching clearly visible) on my behind. Maybe that would have been going too far though. I don't really need a reminder of it anyway. To this day, I swear my butt still hurts whenever the weather changes...or anytime I hear the name Ichiro Suzuki.

As a result of one pitch, I learned a lot of lessons that night, though most required the benefit of time and distance to fully appreciate. Apart from discovering that I could still be vain, even when I was in extreme pain, all the others revolved around control, or rather, the illusion of it.

The first was that I had not been in complete control of the outcome, even though, before that pitch, I'd firmly believed I was. Being alert, focused, and attentive — having my eye on the ball — had not prevented it from hitting me. The second was essentially an inversion of the first: if I had *not* been paying attention, I would have assumed that was why I'd been hit, and I would have blamed myself for it happening, when, in fact, that wasn't true at all. The third lesson was more subtle, but equally important: though I could not prevent the ball from hitting me, I had influenced the ultimate outcome. Because I had been paying attention and was able to turn and bend to protect myself, I had not been as seriously injured as I almost certainly would have been if I hadn't. And the fourth, and final lesson was that sometimes luck is involved — double-sided luck for me in this case: it was unlucky that the ball had been hit right at me, but it was good luck that I'd been standing up to cheer for the final strike of the game. If I'd been sitting in my seat like I had for every other pitch, it would have probably hit me in the face.

As I think back on these lessons all these years later, I realize the first one had kept my hubris in check, the second had kept my culpability in check, and the third had kept me from checking out. The fourth, well, just kept me feeling blessed.

* * *

Not long ago, I came across an ancient Hindi word, *genshai*, which I'll translate in a moment, but I think it is best explained via story:

When I was still in pharmacy school, I applied for a summer internship at the prominent and renowned medical center in my hometown. I was ecstatic when I received a phone call inviting me to come in for an in-person interview and to take a written test. When I arrived at the hospital on the day of the interview, I was excited about the potential job, but also a little nervous. I was greeted by a representative in the lobby, and then taken down a long escalator to the pharmacy department's admin offices located in the basement below. As we slowly descended via the escalator, I couldn't help but notice the large photo mural on the wall in front, and then above, as we passed underneath.

As we were on the escalator, the person escorting me asked, what I thought, was essentially the *"What do you want to be when you grow up?"* question. The medical center was my dream employer. It was large and cutting-edge and had a stellar reputation for service, teaching, research, and patient care. Its clinical pharmacy program was pre-eminent and widely recognized as innovative and forward thinking. I had heard it referred to as mecca, nirvana, even Disneyland. Many considered it *the* place to be a clinical pharmacist. Although I was still a long way from graduation, I wanted to eagerly express my interest and enthusiasm, so without hesitation, I boldly declared that I envisioned working as a critical care pharmacist in the hospital's ICU. This was long before "leaning in" was popular advice, but it was in this spirit that I'd said it. I still remember the pride I felt declaring my bold goal with confidence.

So, I was greatly surprised when he replied sharply in an unexpectedly harsh tone, "Well, you'd be lucky to even get a job here."

His words dripped with ridicule, as if he intended to both put me in my place and let me know I'd overstepped. Embarrassed and a bit demoralized, I scrambled to recover my ego and silently scolded myself. I'd clearly misunderstood the question and had overreached. We were silent for the rest of the ride. I focused on the serenity of the garden and trees in the photo mural that dominated my view, as the sting of his words subsided.

Fast forward many years and experiences later — as the CEO of this same medical center, the medical center I'd grown up in and belonged to — I would ride that escalator down and pass that same photo mural often, while silently and enthusiastically saying to myself "Why, yes, I *am* so lucky to have a job here!"

It's easy to assume I'm sharing this story as an example of triumph, that I'd overcome discouragement and had not let my bruised ego get in the way of achieving my goals. That I'd persevered and risen above. That I'd "shown him!" A little bit of that is true, but that's not why I'm sharing it now.

The far more important lesson I learned in this brief encounter revolved a whole lot less around how it had affected my career, but much more around how his retort had made me feel at the time. It wasn't the harshest thing anyone had ever said to me. It wasn't cruel, and it was far from abusive. But it was memorable because it was unnecessary — and unkind. And though he was long gone by the time I arrived for my first job there, the exchange had motivated me to be more mindful of the impact of my own words on others. Every time I passed it thereafter, the photo mural served as a reminder to never intentionally deflate or demean someone else and to never stomp on someone else's dream.

The lesson from that day grew stronger and more meaningful to me as I rose through the leadership ranks and encountered more and more people who had less positional power than I did. But it deepened even more substantially after the shooting. I had witnessed unspeakable horror, but I'd also witnessed and experienced the extraordinarily positive role that kindness, compassion, and respect played in keeping us unified in the aftermath. Words mattered, whether we were aware of how they'd impacted others at the time, or not.

Not long after the shooting, I came across the word, "genshai," an ancient Hindi word that is loosely translated as "Never treat anyone in a manner that makes them feel small. Including yourself." The discovery of the word solidified the lesson for me, and I committed to practice *genshai* in all my interactions with my friends and family, with my coworkers, and in particular, with those who were vulnerable.

While preparing for the Commencement speech, I realized that I had forgotten along the way that this practice included *myself* as well.

***

The best advice I have ever received when starting a new job and taking on new responsibilities was to stop and take the time to create a 100 Day Plan for the new role. Otherwise, I could be instantly swept up in a whirlwind of busyness and find myself unintentionally hopping from one crisis or urgency to next, and before I knew it, time might get away from me and years would easily slip by. I'd learned from experience that creating a specific plan at the outset helped to clarify my vision, set my intentions, and keep me grounded, especially when the learning curve for the role was steep.

I was on the verge of another new beginning as a leadership consultant, and for the first time since leaving my former role, I felt liberated from the past and energized to contribute again in new and unique ways. I was excited about this next stage of my professional life but also a little scared, and little voices of self-doubt surfaced alongside my reclaimed confidence. Could I successfully re-emerge in a consultant role? Would I still be relevant? Life had moved on while I'd been stuck in the past. For a couple of years, I'd been out of sight; maybe I was now out of mind, too? Would my phone ring?

As I started writing the leadership book, I had long envisioned, I realized it would be impossible to authentically share my perspectives if I sidestepped my experience in leading through and after the trauma. Now that I had recovered, I no longer wanted to avoid the topic, and I no longer thought it was healthy for it to remain unspeakable. Speaking out about the impact it had on me, as a leader and a patient, and on the organization as a whole, could be valuable to others. But the prospect of that was scary, too.

So, it made sense at this juncture to stop and take the time to create a 100 Day Plan for this next phase of my work and revisit the one I'd created the last time I'd assumed a new role. It seemed like a good place to start.

It wasn't the previous 100 Day Plan itself that initially caught my attention. It was the re-discovery of a collection of principles I'd drafted to guide its creation which proved much more useful and valuable in the end. The collection had been part of a handwritten entry in one of my black books dating way back to December 2008. At the top of the page, I'd written a few aspirational questions to frame my thinking: What do you hold sacred? As a leader, what phrases describe your ideal? What values reflect your True North? To be successful in your role as the CEO, what will be called for? Visualize yourself in your role a year from now, how would you like to be described as a leader?

Beneath these questions, ten principles had been jotted down on the page. Although they were simply stated and not finely wordsmithed — I hadn't intended for them to be publicly shared — they had not been hastily scrawled either. Instead, they were neatly listed in numerical order, indicating the careful thought and consideration that had gone into their development. As I reflected years later on the list with the benefit of ample hindsight, I saw that much of it had withstood the test of time and would continue to be relevant to me, regardless of the specific role, rank, title or position that I might hold in the future:

1. Loves the work, heart in it as a servant leader

2. Creates and communicates an inspiring and compelling vision

3. Surrounds herself with exceptional people, supports and facilitates their effectiveness and development

4. Understands part and whole, takes a wide view, both/ and, sees multiple perspectives

5. Moves with speed and power to solve problems — moves towards issues rather than away, relishing rapid pace/high energy

6. Creates business structures, systems, and processes to achieve results that are solidly aligned with goals

7. Honors instincts and has the courage to make tough calls

8. Makes no excuses, no caveats for failure

9. Legacy passer and steward — leaves it better off than she found it

But it was last one that caught me by surprise and, initially, took my breath away:

10. Takes responsibility

I knew that "takes responsibility" had been a long-standing and deeply rooted conviction, but now I was staring at physical evidence from the past that corroborated its existence and importance in my leadership philosophy. It had been a clear expectation. And, at the time, I could only see the value and benefit — the upsides — of taking responsibility. But later, and viewed through the lens of trauma, I'd witnessed and experienced its power to both unite a team and destroy a career.

Since leaving my old role, I'd let go of my old interpretation of "takes responsibility" and established a clearer boundary between what I could take responsibility for, and what I could not, which now took the place of the one that had long ago been blurred.

As I thought more about this tenth principle, I realized I could now take responsibility to correct a mistake I had made long ago. After the shooting, the "Remembrance Garden" was established as the de facto memorial site, but it was left generic and anonymous. I had not been strong enough to properly name the site and to insist that the names of my colleagues, who had been killed in the line of duty, be explicitly listed in tribute.

"Not strong enough" was not said with self-blame, or to make myself feel small. (I'd done that for years already.) I said it because it was true, but I also said it with a much fuller understanding of why I'd been unable to do it at the time, and with new-found self-compassion for the impossible dilemma I'd faced.

I knew, though, that I could not go back in time and reverse that decision, and I knew that I no longer had control over the monument. I no longer had the power and authority to add their names to it. But I still had the ability — and the responsibility — to pay tribute. I could still *stand in* and finally say their names in the dedication of this memoir.

I really had come full circle.

"We shall not cease from exploration

And the end of all our exploring

Will be to arrive where we started

And know the place for the first time."

~ *T.S. Eliot (Four Quartets)*

April 16, 2019

A LOT OF YEARS HAVE PASSED since the day I'd paused, mid-way across the pedestrian bridge connecting the parking structure to the main hospital, to reflect on my first 100 days as CEO. And the future I'd imagined then, was very different than the one that has unfolded.

Within a few months of the Commencement address, I launched a leadership coaching practice and joined a small consulting firm primarily focused on leadership development, teambuilding, and strategic planning. I was not interested in building a big firm or managing a consulting business, per se. I wanted to work directly and personally with leaders and their teams to help them enhance and evolve the culture of their organizations.

As I began to re-emerge and reconnect with other leaders and former colleagues, thankfully, the phone did begin to ring. Day by day, mostly by word-of-mouth, business grew — as did the joy of being of service again — and within a year, my practice was both full — and fulfilling. I was exactly where I needed to be.

But then I began to get calls for help from leaders whose organizations were in the throes or in the aftermath of a traumatic event. Though most had been accustomed to managing crisis or scandal, many reported that the effects of the event had continued to persist far beyond a time period that would be deemed usual and expected. All said that their organizations were struggling to move on and indicated that, at least on some level, distrust, uncertainty, lack of safety (psychological and/or physical), misplaced blame, and internal division were preventing them from healing and full closure. Most reported that the internal reputation of the organization had been harmed, and they worried about the potential for it to be damaged externally as well.

Around the same time, my existing clients were beginning to ask for more information and training on how to prepare for and lead through trauma. Like other consultants, I'm sure, I increasingly encountered stories of how sexual harassment, bullying, threats of violence or mass layoffs, natural disasters, and other major disruptive changes — or the heightened fear of them — were negatively impacting or challenging people's beliefs about the culture of their workplaces.

While a lot has been written about the impact of trauma on individuals, very little has been published to help leaders and their teams specifically navigate the effects of trauma on the organization itself. Studying and reporting on *organizational trauma* is relatively new territory, but I have found several specialists who have published books which combine extensive field research with their expertise in organizational development and culture. I've found their books to be insightful and practical guides for identifying and addressing the issues that emerge when trauma of any kind occurs in an organization. I've referenced them in the Appendix of this one[1-10]. I'm glad to have come across them to support my current work in this area; I only wish they'd been available earlier.

Each of these books resonated with my own lived experience — and reading and studying the work of others naturally caused me to compare and contrast the case studies with our handling of the shooting and its aftermath. We'd done many things very well — largely, because we had a well-defined disaster preparedness plan and, over the years, had gained a lot of experience through practice drills and real events. But there were other areas that we hadn't managed very well, mostly as a result of the unique dynamics and circumstances surrounding the shooting.

Then there were the unforeseeable consequences, the nagging mystery of *why*, the varying degrees and wide range of blame, guilt, and shame that individuals felt, and the overall unspeakability of the trauma — that we simply had not anticipated or been on the lookout for. Without prior experience with this kind of workplace trauma, they hadn't been on any of our checklists or planning documents and we weren't pre-alerted to their potentially damaging impact. In retrospect, they fell into the category of "You Don't Know What You Don't Know."

But on this side of the whole experience and having gone through my own process of recovery, I knew that while trauma can create a lot of chronic fear and stress, there is also a great potential for repair, renewal, and growth, in ways that are paradoxically galvanizing, unifying, and, ultimately, transformational.

I realized I could help others anticipate the impact of trauma on the organization and the individuals within it by speaking about the best practices I'd identified through my own experience and study and what I'd learned as a member of a small (but growing) network of organizational trauma experts. As I began presenting to more and more groups,

I realized that all of these "best practices" (briefly noted in the Appendix) were applicable for leading more effectively through everyday situations and circumstances as well, not just valuable in response to trauma.[11]

In addition to speaking and consulting with leaders and teams, I knew I could also contribute by writing my own book about organizational trauma — not a scholarly textbook or a comprehensive review of the literature, but a personal account — from my perspective as an individual, a patient, and leader.

I'd expected the writing process would be enlightening and therapeutic in many ways for me, too, but it also ended up being the final step in my healing in a way that I hadn't anticipated at all. When I returned to edit the first draft of Part One, I was surprised to discover a vestige of PTSD lurking in almost every sentence: all the trauma scenes had been written in the present tense. I hadn't been recalling or remembering it, but had been, once again, re-living the trauma. Correcting the verb tense was the final act of returning it to the past, where it belongs.

***

April 16, 2019

With relief and appreciation, and a lot of wonder, I whispered three words to myself — words that echoed from long ago and said while on the threshold of a very different milestone. Ten years to the day had passed since that fateful one.

Standing alone in my backyard, I watched the sun peak over the rooftop behind me and begin to illuminate the hillside below. Just like ten years ago, the day was bright and sparkling, but with the gentle coolness of an early spring morning in southern California. I'd chosen to honor the anniversary by spending the morning in quiet contemplation, surrounded by the best bloom in years, after a wetter-than-normal rainy season.

I thought about my colleagues and all that happened on that day and in the decade that followed. And I thought about all that lies ahead. I'd found a new calling, and once again, I imagined the future with enthusiasm and hopefulness. I felt myself relax as I began to fully comprehend how I could continue to make a difference. Though I was encouraged by my growing confidence, I didn't doubt that I'd be frequently tested and challenged in the years to come. Growth, I'd learned, was iterative, often achieved by stretching to the edge and expanding beyond previous limitations. But sometimes it was attained by pausing, contracting, or course-correcting. Wisdom, I had discovered, was knowing which is called for.

As I took it all in, I repeated those three words aloud for reassurance, as confirmation, and in celebration:

"I've got this."

***

———◆———

Dedicated with love and respect to
Kelly Hales and Hugo Bustamante.

———◆———

Appendix: Selected References

While this isn't an academic book or an exhaustive study of the literature pertaining to PTSD, I found the following references and resources valuable and helpful during my search for answers:

1. Bloom, S. L. (2010). *Destroying Sanctuary: The Crisis in Human Delivery Systems.* Oxford University Press.

2. Bloom, S. L. (2013). *Restoring Sanctuary: A New Operating System for Trauma-Informed Systems of Care.* Oxford University Press.

3. Boulanger, G. (2011). *Wounded by Reality: Understanding and Treating Adult Onset Trauma.* Routledge.

4. Friedman, M. J. (n.d.). *PTSD History and Overview.* Retrieved July 2019, from U.S. Department of Veterans Affairs: https://www.ptsd.va.gov/professional/treat/essentials/history_ptsd.asp

5. Gradus, J. L. (n.d.). *Epidemiology of PTSD.* Retrieved July 2019, from U.S. Department of Veterans Affairs: https://www.ptsd.va.gov/professional/treat/essentials/epidemiology.asp

6. Kilpatrick, D. R. (2013). National estimates of exposure to traumatic events and PTSD prevalence using DSM-IV and DSM-5 criteria. *Journal of Traumatic Stress, 26,* 537-547. doi:10.1002/jts21848

7. Morris, D. J. (2016). *The Evil Hours.* Mariner Books.

8. Orange, C. (2010). *Shock Waves: A Practical Guide to Living with a Loved One's PTSD.*

9. van der Kolk, B. M. (2015). *The Body Keeps Score: Brain, Mind, and Body in the Healing of Trauma.* Penguin.

10. Vivian, P. H., Hormann, S. (2013). *Organizational Trauma and Healing.* CreateSpace.

11. Hendel, D. (2018). *Best Practices in Leading through Organizational Trauma.* Presentation Summary:

- Create a disaster response plan and practice the logistics in advance. (I strongly recommend table-top drills for active shooter scenarios, rather than traumatizing people with role playing.)
- Establish a visible process (crisis ops) team that stays intact for the duration of the event and often for weeks after.
- Communicate frequently and in ways that eliminate mystery and don't leave a void.
- Ensure decision-making processes are in place to identify gaps, areas of ambiguity, and conflicts.
- Get expert help for individuals and the organization, both for acute response and to attend to the ongoing impact on culture.
- Take active measures to unite the team and be alert to the potential for division and strife (particularly around search for motive, cause, or who is responsible, even when perpetrator known),
- Address the width and range of blame, shame, and guilt that can exist, and,
- Ensure the trauma does not become taboo and unspeakable.

Acknowledgements

My deepest thanks to my close friends and family who never wavered in their love, support and encouragement.

I am especially grateful to my mother, Barbara O'Keefe, my father, Larry Hendel, my children, Cameron and Jordan, and my wife, Sandy Garza, who never lost faith in me, even when I questioned my own.

Special thanks to my early readers: Kristin Gallagher, Val Green, Shana Hormann, Jill Janov, Elizabeth Landrum, Sue Long, Sue Melvin, Linda Patten, Bob Passero, Deb Richard, and Pat Vivian who provided thoughtful, honest, and insightful feedback.

I'm grateful to my cover artist extraordinaire, Don Sciore, and my publication team, especially editor Suzanne Bowen and my "handler" Nicole Dudley, for their expertise, assistance, and patience with me throughout this process.

Thank you to my business partner, Tammy Sicard, who read (and re-read) this book at each stage of its development, listened to my ideas with care and curiosity, and cheered me on all along the way.

And, finally, I owe an enormous debt of gratitude to Madelynn Rigopoulos and Deborah Ryan who, with wisdom, grace, and gentleness, kept me tethered to reality and grounded in the here-and-now.

About the Author

Dr. Diana Hendel is a healthcare executive with more than 25 years of experience leading at all levels of complex organizations. She served as CEO of one of the largest hospital complexes on the US West Coast and has held key leadership roles in the California Children's Hospital Association, Hospital Association of Southern California, and the Southern California Leadership Council. She has also served as chair of the Greater Long Beach Chamber of Commerce and as the Leader-in-Residence at the Ukleja Center for Ethical Leadership at California State University Long Beach.

Diana has spoken at numerous regional and national conferences on the topics of healthcare and leadership and presented at TEDx SoCal in 2011 ("Childhood Obesity: Small Steps, Big Change"). She earned a B.S. in Biological Sciences from UC Irvine and a Doctor of Pharmacy degree from UC San Francisco.

Currently, Diana is the Senior Partner at Partnership Advantage, a consulting firm dedicated to helping individuals and teams achieve optimal performance and cultivate strong and healthy organizational cultures.

Made in the USA
San Bernardino, CA
31 March 2020